THE ULTIMATE

DECO CHEF DIGITAL

COOKBOOK

EASY AND AFFORDABLE RECIPES TO FRY MOST WANTED FAMILY MEALS

Lela Legrand

CONTENTS

INTRODUCTION

How air frying works

Have you ever seen one of those money machines, where someone steps inside a cylinder, closes the door, and air starts flowing up from the bottom with money flying through the air?

An air fryer is kind of like one of those money machines. When you put your food into the air fryer and close it, hot air circulates around the food and begins to cook it. The temperature of the air fryer and the type of food you're cooking will help determine the amount of time you need to cook your recipe.

The big difference between air frying and traditional deep frying is that air fryers require minimal to no oil to cook the food. The hot air circulating around the food helps to impart that crisp texture instead of the oil involved in deep frying.

A few other technologically advanced mechanisms are involved, but this is the gist of how air frying works. If you're familiar with convection ovens, where hot air is circulated (as opposed to conventional ovens, where the heating element is on the bottom), you'll feel right at home with air frying. An air fryer is essentially a compact convection oven.

If you want to get a bit more science based, what's actually happening from a chemical perspective when food is cooked in an air fryer is something called the Maillard reaction. The Maillard reaction is often referred to as "non-enzymatic browning," or basically a reaction that happens between sugars and amino acids in a recipe that result in the end product taking on a new flavor, texture, and color.

Seeing the benefits of air frying

Air frying is not only a healthier way to cook some more decadent recipes, but it's also efficient. Many popular models of air fryers claim that using an air fryer instead of a deep fryer can lower the fat of the dish by over 75 percent. This actually makes sense when you think about. Let's say you're going to make homemade fried chicken. If you were to use the deep-frying method of cooking, you'd traditionally need more than 3 cups of oil to cover the chicken to allow the cooking to ensue. On the other hand, if you were to use the air frying method, you'd need less than a tablespoon of oil.

Here are a few other benefits of air frying:

- **Air fryers can promote weight loss (for certain individuals).**

For individuals who currently have a highly processed diet filled with deep-fried foods, switching to air frying will certainly help with reducing caloric intake. A reduction in caloric intake will inevitably result in weight loss.

- **Air fryers can increase consumption of healthy foods, like fish, shrimp, and produce.**

Eating seafood at least twice a week, as well as increasing your consumption of fruits and vegetables, is highly recommended. If you struggle with getting your family to eat more of these foods on a regular basis, then air frying may be the best way to change their appetites (and minds!).

Not only can you put a light crunchy coating of heart-healthy nuts on some of your fried seafood favorites and cook them in the air fryer, but you can do the same with new herbs, spices, and vegetables! This is a great way to explore new vegetables and flavors in your kitchen, too.

- **Air fryers are safer (for the most part) than deep fryers.**

Deep frying can cause splatters of exceptionally hot oil all over your kitchen. Air fryers get super-hot as well, but they don't splatter in the same way a deep fryer does.

As long as you practice important safety measures when taking foods in and out of your fryer (for example, don't put your hands on the fryer basket), you can feel secure in using your fryer.

- **Air fryers can reduce the risk of potentially harmful agents on certain foods.**

A compound called *acrylamide* naturally forms on carbohydrate-rich foods (those traditionally deep-fried foods like french fries, breaded meats, and so on) when cooked at high temperatures. Some studies have found an association between acrylamide and cancer. The jury's still out on whether acrylamide actually *causes* cancer. What you need to know is that air frying is associated with a *decreased* amount of this compound as compared to deep frying, but some may still be present. We firmly believe in balance and moderation. We wouldn't recommend you eat french fries (even air-fried ones) daily.

- **Air fryers can reduce the risk of preventable diseases affected by diet and nutrition.**

This varies depending on many factors like your genetics and current lifestyle habits (such as nutrition and exercise). That said, if your diet is heavy in processed, fried foods, the air fryer may just be the ticket to enjoying the foods you crave in a new, exciting, and healthier way. Not only can you modify the amount of sodium in your recipes and use more fresh herbs and spices to give flavor to the food instead of salt, but you can also increase the fiber in your diet while including more plants in your meal plan.

Using Your Deco Chef Digital Air Fryer

Each make and model of air fryer has its own instructions, but air fryers don't require extensive knowledge to operate. We recommend that you start by reading the manual that came with your Deco Chef Digital air fryer and getting to know your particular machine.

With that said, here are a few basic steps that work for Your Deco Chef Digital Air Fryer:

1. Clean the air fryer basket and accessories with hot soapy water and dry with a dish towel before use.
2. Plug in your air fryer and preheat it.

   This allows the machine time to get to temperature before you actually put the recipe inside.
3. Select Air Fry as the function.
4. Place your food on the wire rack or trivet, securely seal or close the drawer, and begin to air fry.
5. Check the food as applicable, following the recipe instructions.
6. When cooking completes, press Cancel and unplug the air fryer.

Caring for Your Deco Chef Digital Air Fryer

You don't have to invest in any specific detergent or cleanser to keep your Deco Chef Digital air fryer smelling like new. Use this section as your guide to keep your new kitchen appliance in tip-top shape so you can use it for years to come. Cleaning your Deco Chef Digital air fryer is actually a really simple task. With a little elbow grease, some regular dish detergent, and hot water, your air fryer will come back to life, even with the toughest of buildup.

We've experimented with various makes and models and had our fair share of epic disasters in our air fryers, but guess what? After letting the basket and/or tray cool, we were easily able to get the buildup off with a regular kitchen sponge and hot soapy water.

Plus, even when switching between seafood and a decadent dessert, the air fryer doesn't require a deep clean.

Wipe down the outside of your fryer after each use. A hot, soapy towel is all that's necessary. This helps get off any grease or food particles that may have latched on during cooking.

Your Deco Chef Digital air fryer manual may say that the parts to wash are dishwasher safe, but we recommend that you hand wash them instead. Why? Because hand washing will keep your air fryer in better shape than putting it through the wear and tear of the dishwasher. Just spend 5 minutes to give it a thorough hand wash after each use, and you'll have a properly working air fryer for years to come.

APPETIZERS AND SNACKS

Crunchy Tortellini Bites

Servings: 5

Cooking Time: 10 Minutes

Ingredients:

- 10 ounces (about 2½ cups) Cheese tortellini
- ⅓ cup Yellow cornmeal
- ⅓ cup Seasoned Italian-style dried bread crumbs
- ⅓ cup (about 1 ounce) Finely grated Parmesan cheese
- 1 Large egg
- Olive oil spray

Directions:

1. Bring a large pot of water to a boil over high heat. Add the tortellini and cook for 3 minutes. Drain in a colander set in the sink, then spread out the tortellini on a large baking sheet and cool for 15 minutes.
2. Preheat the air fryer to 400°F.
3. Mix the cornmeal, bread crumbs, and cheese in a large zip-closed plastic bag.
4. Whisk the egg in a medium bowl until uniform. Add the tortellini and toss well to coat, even along the inside curve of the pasta. Use a slotted spoon or kitchen tongs to transfer 5 or 6 tortellini to the plastic bag, seal, and shake gently to coat thoroughly and evenly. Set the coated tortellini aside on a cutting board and continue coating the rest in the same way.
5. Generously coat the tortellini on all sides with the olive oil spray, then set them in one layer in the basket. Air-fry undisturbed for 10 minutes, gently tossing the basket and rearranging the tortellini at the 4- and 7-minute marks, until brown and crisp.
6. Pour the contents of the basket onto a wire rack. Cool for 5 minutes before serving.

Homemade French Fries

Servings: 2

Cooking Time: 25 Minutes

Ingredients:

- 2 to 3 russet potatoes, peeled and cut into ½-inch sticks
- 2 to 3 teaspoons olive or vegetable oil
- salt

Directions:

1. Bring a large saucepan of salted water to a boil on the stovetop while you peel and cut the potatoes. Blanch the potatoes in the boiling salted water for 4 minutes while you Preheat the air fryer to 400°F. Strain the potatoes and rinse them with cold water. Dry them well with a clean kitchen towel.
2. Toss the dried potato sticks gently with the oil and place them in the air fryer basket. Air-fry for 25 minutes, shaking the basket a few times while the fries cook to help them brown evenly. Season the fries with salt mid-way through cooking and serve them warm with tomato ketchup, Sriracha mayonnaise or a mix of lemon zest, Parmesan cheese and parsley.

Honey-mustard Chicken Wings

Servings: 2

Cooking Time: 14 Minutes

Ingredients:

- 2 pounds chicken wings
- salt and freshly ground black pepper
- 2 tablespoons butter
- ¼ cup honey
- ¼ cup spicy brown mustard
- pinch ground cayenne pepper
- 2 teaspoons Worcestershire sauce

Directions:

1. Prepare the chicken wings by cutting off the wing tips and discarding (or freezing for chicken stock). Divide the drumettes from the wingettes by cutting through the joint. Place the chicken wing pieces in a large bowl.
2. Preheat the air fryer to 400°F.
3. Season the wings with salt and freshly ground black pepper and air-fry the wings in two batches for 10 minutes per batch, shaking the basket half way through the cooking process.
4. While the wings are air-frying, combine the remaining ingredients in a small saucepan over low heat.
5. When both batches are done, toss all the wings with the honey-mustard sauce and toss them all back into the basket for another 4 minutes to heat through and finish cooking. Give the basket a good shake part way through the cooking process to redistribute the wings. Remove the wings from the air fryer and serve.

Cheese Wafers

Servings: 4

Cooking Time: 6 Minutes Per Batch

Ingredients:

- 4 ounces sharp Cheddar cheese, grated
- ¼ cup butter
- ½ cup flour
- ¼ teaspoon salt
- ½ cup crisp rice cereal
- oil for misting or cooking spray

Directions:

1. Cream the butter and grated cheese together. You can do it by hand, but using a stand mixer is faster and easier.
2. Sift flour and salt together. Add it to the cheese mixture and mix until well blended.
3. Stir in cereal.
4. Place dough on wax paper and shape into a long roll about 1 inch in diameter. Wrap well with the wax paper and chill for at least 4 hours.
5. When ready to cook, preheat air fryer to 360°F.
6. Cut cheese roll into ¼-inch slices.
7. Spray air fryer basket with oil or cooking spray and place slices in a single layer, close but not touching.
8. Cook for 6minutes or until golden brown. When done, place them on paper towels to cool.
9. Repeat previous step to cook remaining cheese bites.

Zucchini Fritters

Servings: 8

Cooking Time: 10 Minutes

Ingredients:

- 2 cups grated zucchini
- ½ teaspoon sea salt
- 1 egg
- ½ teaspoon garlic powder
- ¼ teaspoon onion powder
- ¼ cup grated Parmesan cheese
- ½ cup all-purpose flour
- ¼ teaspoon baking powder
- ½ cup Greek yogurt or sour cream
- ½ lime, juiced
- ¼ cup chopped cilantro
- ¼ teaspoon ground cumin
- ¼ teaspoon salt

Directions:

1. Preheat the air fryer to 360°F.
2. In a large colander, place a kitchen towel. Inside the towel, place the grated zucchini and sprinkle the sea salt over the top. Let the zucchini sit for 5 minutes; then, using the towel, squeeze dry the zucchini.
3. In a medium bowl, mix together the egg, garlic powder, onion powder, Parmesan cheese, flour, and baking powder. Add in the grated zucchini, and stir until completely combined.
4. Pierce a piece of parchment paper with a fork 4 to 6 times. Place the parchment paper into the air fryer basket. Using a tablespoon, place 6 to 8 heaping tablespoons of fritter batter onto the parchment paper. Spray the fritters with cooking spray and cook for 5 minutes, turn the fritters over, and cook another 5 minutes.
5. Meanwhile, while the fritters are cooking, make the sauce. In a small bowl, whisk together the Greek yogurt or sour cream, lime juice, cilantro, cumin, and salt.
6. Repeat Steps 2–4 with the remaining batter.

Spicy Chicken And Pepper Jack Cheese Bites

Servings: 8

Cooking Time: 8 Minutes

Ingredients:

- 8 ounces cream cheese, softened
- 2 cups grated pepper jack cheese
- 1 Jalapeño pepper, diced
- 2 scallions, minced
- 1 teaspoon paprika
- 2 teaspoons salt, divided
- 3 cups shredded cooked chicken
- ¼ cup all-purpose flour*
- 2 eggs, lightly beaten
- 1 cup panko breadcrumbs*
- olive oil, in a spray bottle
- salsa

Directions:

1. Beat the cream cheese in a bowl until it is smooth and easy to stir. Add the pepper jack cheese, Jalapeño pepper, scallions, paprika and 1 teaspoon of salt. Fold in the shredded cooked chicken and combine well. Roll this mixture into 1-inch balls.
2. Set up a dredging station with three shallow dishes. Place the flour into one shallow dish. Place the eggs into a second shallow dish. Finally, combine the panko breadcrumbs and remaining teaspoon of salt in a third dish.
3. Coat the chicken cheese balls by rolling each ball in the flour first, then dip them into the eggs and finally roll them in the panko breadcrumbs to coat all sides. Refrigerate for at least 30 minutes.
4. Preheat the air fryer to 400°F.
5. Spray the chicken cheese balls with oil and air-fry in batches for 8 minutes. Shake the basket a few times throughout the cooking process to help the balls brown evenly.
6. Serve hot with salsa on the side.

Corn Tortilla Chips

Servings: 4

Cooking Time: 12 Minutes

Ingredients:

- Eight 6-inch corn tortillas
- ½ teaspoon sea salt
- ¼ teaspoon ground cumin
- ¼ teaspoon chili powder
- ¼ teaspoon garlic powder
- ⅛ teaspoon onion powder
- 1 tablespoon avocado oil

Directions:

1. Cut each corn tortilla into quarters, creating 32 chips in total.
2. Preheat the air fryer to 350°F.
3. In a small bowl, mix together the sea salt, cumin, chili powder, garlic powder, and onion powder.
4. Spray or brush one side of the tortillas with avocado oil. Sprinkle the seasoning mixture evenly over the oiled side of the chips.
5. Working in batches, place half the chips in the air fryer basket. Cook for 8 minutes, shake the basket, and cook another 2 to 4 minutes, checking for crispness. When the chips are golden brown, spread them out onto paper towels and allow them to cool for 3 minutes before serving. Repeat with the remaining chips.

Crab Rangoon Dip With Wonton Chips

Servings: 6

Cooking Time: 18 Minutes

Ingredients:

- Wonton Chips:
- 1 (12-ounce) package wonton wrappers
- vegetable oil
- sea salt
- Crab Rangoon Dip:
- 8 ounces cream cheese, softened
- ¾ cup sour cream
- 1 teaspoon Worcestershire sauce
- 1½ teaspoons soy sauce
- 1 teaspoon sesame oil
- ⅛ teaspoon ground cayenne pepper
- ¼ teaspoon salt
- freshly ground black pepper
- 8 ounces cooked crabmeat
- 1 cup grated white Cheddar cheese
- ⅓ cup chopped scallions
- paprika (for garnish)

Directions:

1. Cut the wonton wrappers in half diagonally to form triangles. Working in batches, lay the wonton triangles on a flat surface and brush or spray both sides with vegetable oil.
2. Preheat the air fryer to 370°F.
3. Place about 10 to 12 wonton triangles in the air fryer basket, letting them overlap slightly. Air-fry for just 2 minutes, shaking the basket halfway through the cooking time. Transfer the wonton chips to a large bowl and season immediately with sea salt. (You'll hear the chips start to spin around in the air fryer when they are almost done.) Repeat with the rest of wontons (keeping those fishing hands at bay!).
4. To make the dip, combine the cream cheese, sour cream, Worcestershire sauce, soy sauce, sesame oil, cayenne pepper, salt, and freshly ground black pepper in a bowl. Mix well and then fold in the crabmeat, Cheddar cheese, and scallions.
5. Transfer the dip to a 7-inch ceramic baking pan or shallow casserole dish. Sprinkle paprika on top and cover the dish with aluminum foil. Lower the dish into the air fryer basket using a sling made of aluminum foil (fold a piece of aluminum foil into a strip about 2-inches wide by 24-inches long). Air-fry for 11 minutes. Remove the aluminum foil and air-fry for another 5 minutes to finish cooking and brown the top. Serve hot with the wonton chips.

BEEF， PORK & LAMB RECIPES

Steakhouse Filets Mignons

Servings: 3

Cooking Time: 12-15 Minutes

Ingredients:

- ¾ ounce Dried porcini mushrooms
- ¼ teaspoon Granulated white sugar
- ¼ teaspoon Ground white pepper
- ¼ teaspoon Table salt
- 6 ¼-pound filets mignons or beef tenderloin steaks
- 6 Thin-cut bacon strips (gluten-free, if a concern)

Directions:

1. Preheat the air fryer to 400°F.
2. Grind the dried mushrooms in a clean spice grinder until powdery. Add the sugar, white pepper, and salt. Grind to blend.
3. Rub this mushroom mixture into both cut sides of each filet. Wrap the circumference of each filet with a strip of bacon. (It will loop around the beef about 1½ times.)
4. Set the filets mignons in the basket on their sides with the bacon seam side down. Do not let the filets touch; keep at least ¼ inch open between them. Air-fry undisturbed for 12 minutes for rare, or until an instant-read meat thermometer inserted into the center of a filet registers 125°F (not USDA-approved); 13 minutes for medium-rare, or until an instant-read meat thermometer inserted into the center of a filet registers 132°F (not USDA-approved); or 15 minutes for medium, or until an instant-read meat thermometer inserted into the center of a filet registers 145°F (USDA-approved).
5. Use kitchen tongs to transfer the filets to a wire rack, setting them cut side down. Cool for 5 minutes before serving.

Greek Pita Pockets

Servings: 4

Cooking Time: 7 Minutes

Ingredients:

- Dressing
- 1 cup plain yogurt
- 1 tablespoon lemon juice
- 1 teaspoon dried dill weed, crushed
- 1 teaspoon ground oregano
- ½ teaspoon salt
- Meatballs
- ½ pound ground lamb
- 1 tablespoon diced onion
- 1 teaspoon dried parsley
- 1 teaspoon dried dill weed, crushed
- ¼ teaspoon oregano
- ¼ teaspoon coriander
- ¼ teaspoon ground cumin
- ¼ teaspoon salt
- 4 pita halves
- Suggested Toppings
- red onion, slivered
- seedless cucumber, thinly sliced
- crumbled Feta cheese
- sliced black olives
- chopped fresh peppers

Directions:

1. Stir dressing ingredients together and refrigerate while preparing lamb.
2. Combine all meatball ingredients in a large bowl and stir to distribute seasonings.
3. Shape meat mixture into 12 small meatballs, rounded or slightly flattened if you prefer.
4. Cook at 390°F for 7minutes, until well done. Remove and drain on paper towels.
5. To serve, pile meatballs and your choice of toppings in pita pockets and drizzle with dressing.

Pork Taco Gorditas

Servings: 4

Cooking Time: 21 Minutes

Ingredients:

- 1 pound lean ground pork
- 2 tablespoons chili powder
- 2 tablespoons ground cumin
- 1 teaspoon dried oregano
- 2 teaspoons paprika
- 1 teaspoon garlic powder
- ½ cup water
- 1 (15-ounce) can pinto beans, drained and rinsed
- ½ cup taco sauce
- salt and freshly ground black pepper
- 2 cups grated Cheddar cheese
- 5 (12-inch) flour tortillas
- 4 (8-inch) crispy corn tortilla shells
- 4 cups shredded lettuce
- 1 tomato, diced
- ⅓ cup sliced black olives
- sour cream, for serving
- tomato salsa, for serving

Directions:

1. Preheat the air fryer to 400°F.
2. Place the ground pork in the air fryer basket and air-fry at 400°F for 10 minutes, stirring a few times during the cooking process to gently break up the meat. Combine the chili powder, cumin, oregano, paprika, garlic powder and water in a small bowl. Stir the spice mixture into the browned pork. Stir in the beans and taco sauce and air-fry for an additional minute. Transfer the pork mixture to a bowl. Season to taste with salt and freshly ground black pepper.
3. Sprinkle ½ cup of the shredded cheese in the center of four of the flour tortillas, making sure to leave a 2-inch border around the edge free of cheese and filling. Divide the pork mixture among the four tortillas, placing it on top of the cheese. Place a crunchy corn tortilla on top of the pork and top with shredded lettuce, diced tomatoes, and black olives. Cut the remaining flour tortilla into 4 quarters. These quarters of tortilla will serve as the bottom of the gordita. Place one quarter tortilla on top of each gordita and fold the edges of the bottom flour tortilla up over the sides, enclosing the filling. While holding the seams down, brush the bottom of the gordita with olive oil and place the seam side down on the countertop while you finish the remaining three gorditas.
4. Preheat the air fryer to 380°F.
5. Air-fry one gordita at a time. Transfer the gordita carefully to the air fryer basket, seam side down. Brush or spray the top tortilla with oil and air-fry for 5 minutes. Carefully turn the gordita over and air-fry for an additional 5 minutes, until both sides are browned. When finished air frying all four gorditas, layer them back into the air fryer for an additional minute to make sure they are all warm before serving with sour cream and salsa.

Brie And Cranberry Burgers

Servings: 3

Cooking Time: 9 Minutes

Ingredients:

- 1 pound ground beef (80% lean)
- 1 tablespoon chopped fresh thyme
- 1 tablespoon Worcestershire sauce
- ½ teaspoon salt
- freshly ground black pepper
- 1 (4-ounce) wheel of Brie cheese, sliced
- handful of arugula
- 3 or 4 brioche hamburger buns (or potato hamburger buns), toasted
- ¼ to ½ cup whole berry cranberry sauce

Directions:

1. Combine the beef, thyme, Worcestershire sauce, salt and pepper together in a large bowl and mix well. Divide the meat into 4 (¼-pound) portions or 3 larger portions and then form them into burger patties, being careful not to over-handle the meat.
2. Preheat the air fryer to 390°F and pour a little water into the bottom of the air fryer drawer. (This will help prevent the grease that drips into the bottom drawer from burning and smoking.)
3. Transfer the burgers to the air fryer basket. Air-fry the burgers at 390°F for 5 minutes. Flip the burgers over and air-fry for another 2 minutes. Top each burger with a couple slices of brie and air-fry for another minute or two, just to soften the cheese.
4. Build the burgers by placing a few leaves of arugula on the bottom bun, adding the burger and a spoonful of cranberry sauce on top. Top with the other half of the hamburger bun and enjoy.

Better-than-chinese-take-out Sesame Beef

Servings: 4

Cooking Time: 14 Minutes

Ingredients:

- 1¼ pounds Beef flank steak
- 2½ tablespoons Regular or low-sodium soy sauce or gluten-free tamari sauce
- 2 tablespoons Toasted sesame oil
- 2½ teaspoons Cornstarch
- 1 pound 2 ounces (about 4½ cups) Frozen mixed vegetables for stir-fry, thawed, seasoning packet discarded
- 3 tablespoons Unseasoned rice vinegar (see here)
- 3 tablespoons Thai sweet chili sauce
- 2 tablespoons Light brown sugar
- 2 tablespoons White sesame seeds
- 2 teaspoons Water
- Vegetable oil spray
- 1½ tablespoons Minced peeled fresh ginger
- 1 tablespoon Minced garlic

Directions:

1. Set the flank steak on a cutting board and run your clean fingers across it to figure out which way the meat's fibers are running. (Usually, they run the long way from end to end, or perhaps slightly at an angle lengthwise along the cut.) Cut the flank steak into three pieces parallel to the meat's grain. Then cut each of these pieces into ½-inch-wide strips against the grain.
2. Put the meat strips in a large bowl. For a small batch, add 2 teaspoons of the soy or tamari sauce, 2 teaspoons of the sesame oil, and ½ teaspoon of the cornstarch; for a medium batch, add 1 tablespoon of the soy or tamari sauce, 1 tablespoon of the sesame oil, and 1 teaspoon of the cornstarch; and for a large batch, add 1½ tablespoons of the soy or tamari sauce, 1½ tablespoons of the sesame oil, and 1½ teaspoons of the cornstarch. Toss well until the meat is thoroughly coated in the marinade. Set aside at room temperature.
3. Preheat the air fryer to 400°F.
4. When the machine is at temperature, place the beef strips in the basket in as close to one layer as possible. The strips will overlap or even cover each other. Air-fry for 10 minutes, tossing and rearranging the strips three times so that the covered parts get exposed, until browned and even a little crisp. Pour the strips into a clean bowl.
5. Spread the vegetables in the basket and air-fry undisturbed for 4 minutes, just until they are heated through and somewhat softened. Pour these into the bowl with the meat strips. Turn off the air fryer.
6. Whisk the rice vinegar, sweet chili sauce, brown sugar, sesame seeds, the remaining soy sauce, and the remaining sesame oil in a small bowl until well combined. For a small batch, whisk the remaining 1 teaspoon cornstarch with the water in a second small bowl to make a smooth slurry; for medium batch, whisk the remaining 1½ teaspoons cornstarch with the water in a second small bowl to make a smooth

slurry; and for a large batch, whisk the remaining 2 teaspoons cornstarch with the water in a second small bowl to make a smooth slurry.

7. Generously coat the inside of a large wok with vegetable oil spray, then set the wok over high heat for a few minutes. Add the ginger and garlic; stir-fry for 10 seconds or so, just until fragrant. Add the meat and vegetables; stir-fry for 1 minute to heat through.

8. Add the rice vinegar mixture and continue stir-frying until the sauce is bubbling, less than 1 minute. Add the cornstarch slurry and stir-fry until the sauce has thickened, just a few seconds. Remove the wok from the heat and serve hot.

Orange Glazed Pork Tenderloin

Servings: 3 Cooking Time: 23 Minutes

Ingredients:

- 2 tablespoons brown sugar
- 2 teaspoons cornstarch
- 2 teaspoons Dijon mustard
- ½ cup orange juice
- ½ teaspoon soy sauce*
- 2 teaspoons grated fresh ginger
- ¼ cup white wine
- zest of 1 orange
- 1 pound pork tenderloin
- salt and freshly ground black pepper
- oranges, halved (for garnish)
- fresh parsley or other green herb (for garnish)

Directions:

1. Combine the brown sugar, cornstarch, Dijon mustard, orange juice, soy sauce, ginger, white wine and orange zest in a small saucepan and bring the mixture to a boil on the stovetop. Lower the heat and simmer while you cook the pork tenderloin or until the sauce has thickened.
2. Preheat the air fryer to 370°F.
3. Season all sides of the pork tenderloin with salt and freshly ground black pepper. Transfer the tenderloin to the air fryer basket, bending the pork into a wide "U" shape if necessary to fit in the basket. Air-fry at 370°F for 20 to 23 minutes, or until the internal temperature reaches 145°F. Flip the tenderloin over halfway through the cooking process and baste with the sauce.
4. Transfer the tenderloin to a cutting board and let it rest for 5 minutes. Slice the pork at a slight angle and serve immediately with orange halves and fresh herbs to dress it up. Drizzle any remaining glaze over the top.

Better-than-chinese-take-out Pork Ribs

Servings: 3

Cooking Time: 35 Minutes

Ingredients:

- 1½ tablespoons Hoisin sauce (see here; gluten-free, if a concern)
- 1½ tablespoons Regular or low-sodium soy sauce or gluten-free tamari sauce
- 1½ tablespoons Shaoxing (Chinese cooking rice wine), dry sherry, or white grape juice
- 1½ teaspoons Minced garlic
- ¾ teaspoon Ground dried ginger
- ¾ teaspoon Ground white pepper
- 1½ pounds Pork baby back rib rack(s), cut into 2-bone pieces

Directions:

1. Mix the hoisin sauce, soy or tamari sauce, Shaoxing or its substitute, garlic, ginger, and white pepper in a large bowl. Add the rib sections and stir well to coat. Cover and refrigerate for at least 2 hours or up to 24 hours, stirring the rib sections in the marinade occasionally.
2. Preheat the air fryer to 350°F . Set the ribs in their bowl on the counter as the machine heats.
3. When the machine is at temperature, set the rib pieces on their sides in a single layer in the basket with as much air space between them as possible. Air-fry for 35 minutes, turning and rearranging the pieces once, until deeply browned and sizzling.
4. Use kitchen tongs to transfer the rib pieces to a large serving bowl or platter. Wait a minute or two before serving them so the meat can reabsorb some of its own juices.

Kielbasa Chunks With Pineapple & Peppers

Servings: 2

Cooking Time: 10 Minutes

Ingredients:

- ¾ pound kielbasa sausage
- 1 cup bell pepper chunks (any color)
- 1 8-ounce can pineapple chunks in juice, drained
- 1 tablespoon barbeque seasoning
- 1 tablespoon soy sauce
- cooking spray

Directions:

1. Cut sausage into ½-inch slices.
2. In a medium bowl, toss all ingredients together.
3. Spray air fryer basket with nonstick cooking spray.
4. Pour sausage mixture into the basket.
5. Cook at 390°F for approximately 5minutes. Shake basket and cook an additional 5minutes.

Lamb Koftas Meatballs

Servings: 3

Cooking Time: 8 Minutes

Ingredients:

- 1 pound ground lamb
- 1 teaspoon ground cumin
- 1 teaspoon ground coriander
- 2 tablespoons chopped fresh mint
- 1 egg, beaten
- ½ teaspoon salt
- freshly ground black pepper

Directions:

1. Combine all ingredients in a bowl and mix together well. Divide the mixture into 10 portions. Roll each portion into a ball and then by cupping the meatball in your hand, shape it into an oval.
2. Preheat the air fryer to 400°F.
3. Air-fry the koftas for 8 minutes.
4. Serve warm with the cucumber-yogurt dip.

Lamb Burger With Feta And Olives

Servings: 3

Cooking Time: 16 Minutes

Ingredients:

- 2 teaspoons olive oil
- ⅓ onion, finely chopped
- 1 clove garlic, minced
- 1 pound ground lamb
- 2 tablespoons fresh parsley, finely chopped
- 1½ teaspoons fresh oregano, finely chopped
- ½ cup black olives, finely chopped
- ⅓ cup crumbled feta cheese
- ½ teaspoon salt
- freshly ground black pepper
- 4 thick pita breads
- toppings and condiments

Directions:

1. Preheat a medium skillet over medium-high heat on the stovetop. Add the olive oil and cook the onion until tender, but not browned – about 4 to 5 minutes. Add the garlic and cook for another minute. Transfer the onion and garlic to a mixing bowl and add the ground lamb, parsley, oregano, olives, feta cheese, salt and pepper. Gently mix the ingredients together.
2. Divide the mixture into 3 or 4 equal portions and then form the hamburgers, being careful not to over-handle the meat. One good way to do this is to throw the meat back and forth between your hands like a baseball, packing the meat each time you catch it. Flatten the balls into patties, making an indentation in the center of each patty. Flatten the sides of the patties as well to make it easier to fit them into the air fryer basket.
3. Preheat the air fryer to 370°F.
4. If you don't have room for all four burgers, air-fry two or three burgers at a time for 8 minutes at 370°F. Flip the burgers over and air-fry for another 8 minutes. If you cooked your burgers in batches, return the first batch of burgers to the air fryer for the last two minutes of cooking to re-heat. This should give you a medium-well burger. If you'd prefer a medium-rare burger, shorten the cooking time to about 13 minutes. Remove the burgers to a resting plate and let the burgers rest for a few minutes before dressing and serving.
5. While the burgers are resting, toast the pita breads in the air fryer for 2 minutes. Tuck the burgers into the toasted pita breads, or wrap the pitas around the burgers and serve with a tzatziki sauce or some mayonnaise.

Pepperoni Pockets

Servings: 4

Cooking Time: 8 Minutes

Ingredients:

- 4 bread slices, 1-inch thick
- olive oil for misting
- 24 slices pepperoni (about 2 ounces)
- 1 ounce roasted red peppers, drained and patted dry
- 1 ounce Pepper Jack cheese cut into 4 slices
- pizza sauce (optional)

Directions:

1. Spray both sides of bread slices with olive oil.
2. Stand slices upright and cut a deep slit in the top to create a pocket—almost to the bottom crust but not all the way through.
3. Stuff each bread pocket with 6 slices of pepperoni, a large strip of roasted red pepper, and a slice of cheese.
4. Place bread pockets in air fryer basket, standing up. Cook at 360°F for 8 minutes, until filling is heated through and bread is lightly browned. Serve while hot as is or with pizza sauce for dipping.

Barbecue Country-style Pork Ribs

Servings: 3

Cooking Time: 30 Minutes

Ingredients:

- 3 8-ounce boneless country-style pork ribs
- 1½ teaspoons Mild smoked paprika
- 1½ teaspoons Light brown sugar
- ¾ teaspoon Onion powder
- ¾ teaspoon Ground black pepper
- ¼ teaspoon Table salt
- Vegetable oil spray

Directions:

1. Preheat the air fryer to 350°F . Set the ribs in a bowl on the counter as the machine heats.
2. Mix the smoked paprika, brown sugar, onion powder, pepper, and salt in a small bowl until well combined. Rub this mixture over all the surfaces of the country-style ribs. Generously coat the country-style ribs with vegetable oil spray.
3. Set the ribs in the basket with as much air space between them as possible. Air-fry undisturbed for 30 minutes, or until browned and sizzling and an instant-read meat thermometer inserted into one rib registers at least 145°F.
4. Use kitchen tongs to transfer the country-style ribs to a wire rack. Cool for 5 minutes before serving.

POULTRY RECIPES

Peanut Butter-barbeque Chicken

Servings: 4

Cooking Time: 20 Minutes

Ingredients:

- 1 pound boneless, skinless chicken thighs
- salt and pepper
- 1 large orange
- ½ cup barbeque sauce
- 2 tablespoons smooth peanut butter
- 2 tablespoons chopped peanuts for garnish (optional)
- cooking spray

Directions:

1. Season chicken with salt and pepper to taste. Place in a shallow dish or plastic bag.
2. Grate orange peel, squeeze orange and reserve 1 tablespoon of juice for the sauce.
3. Pour remaining juice over chicken and marinate for 30minutes.
4. Mix together the reserved 1 tablespoon of orange juice, barbeque sauce, peanut butter, and 1 teaspoon grated orange peel.
5. Place ¼ cup of sauce mixture in a small bowl for basting. Set remaining sauce aside to serve with cooked chicken.
6. Preheat air fryer to 360°F. Spray basket with nonstick cooking spray.
7. Remove chicken from marinade, letting excess drip off. Place in air fryer basket and cook for 5minutes. Turn chicken over and cook 5minutes longer.
8. Brush both sides of chicken lightly with sauce.
9. Cook chicken 5minutes, then turn thighs one more time, again brushing both sides lightly with sauce. Cook for 5 moreminutes or until chicken is done and juices run clear.
10. Serve chicken with remaining sauce on the side and garnish with chopped peanuts if you like.

Peachy Chicken Chunks With Cherries

Servings: 4

Cooking Time: 16 Minutes

Ingredients:

- ⅓ cup peach preserves
- 1 teaspoon ground rosemary
- ½ teaspoon black pepper
- ½ teaspoon salt
- ½ teaspoon marjoram
- 1 teaspoon light olive oil
- 1 pound boneless chicken breasts, cut in 1½-inch chunks
- oil for misting or cooking spray
- 10-ounce package frozen unsweetened dark cherries, thawed and drained

Directions:

1. In a medium bowl, mix together peach preserves, rosemary, pepper, salt, marjoram, and olive oil.
2. Stir in chicken chunks and toss to coat well with the preserve mixture.
3. Spray air fryer basket with oil or cooking spray and lay chicken chunks in basket.
4. Cook at 390°F for 7minutes. Stir. Cook for 8 more minutes or until chicken juices run clear.
5. When chicken has cooked through, scatter the cherries over and cook for additional minute to heat cherries.

Taquitos

Servings: 12

Cooking Time: 6 Minutes Per Batch

Ingredients:

- 1 teaspoon butter
- 2 tablespoons chopped green onions
- 1 cup cooked chicken, shredded
- 2 tablespoons chopped green chiles
- 2 ounces Pepper Jack cheese, shredded
- 4 tablespoons salsa
- ½ teaspoon lime juice
- ¼ teaspoon cumin
- ½ teaspoon chile powder
- ⅛ teaspoon garlic powder
- 12 corn tortillas
- oil for misting or cooking spray

Directions:

1. Melt butter in a saucepan over medium heat. Add green onions and sauté a minute or two, until tender.
2. Remove from heat and stir in the chicken, green chiles, cheese, salsa, lime juice, and seasonings.
3. Preheat air fryer to 390°F.
4. To soften refrigerated tortillas, wrap in damp paper towels and microwave for 30 to 60 seconds, until slightly warmed.
5. Remove one tortilla at a time, keeping others covered with the damp paper towels. Place a heaping tablespoon of filling into tortilla, roll up and secure with toothpick. Spray all sides with oil or cooking spray.
6. Place taquitos in air fryer basket, either in a single layer or stacked. To stack, leave plenty of space between taquitos and alternate the direction of the layers, 4 on the bottom lengthwise, then 4 more on top crosswise.
7. Cook for 6minutes or until brown and crispy.
8. Repeat steps 6 and 7 to cook remaining taquitos.
9. Serve hot with guacamole, sour cream, salsa or all three!

Crispy "fried" Chicken

Servings: 4

Cooking Time: 14 Minutes

Ingredients:

- ¾ cup all-purpose flour
- ½ teaspoon paprika
- ¼ teaspoon black pepper
- ¼ teaspoon salt
- 2 large eggs
- 1½ cups panko breadcrumbs
- 1 pound boneless, skinless chicken tenders

Directions:

1. Preheat the air fryer to 400°F.
2. In a shallow bowl, mix the flour with the paprika, pepper, and salt.
3. In a separate bowl, whisk the eggs; set aside.
4. In a third bowl, place the breadcrumbs.
5. Liberally spray the air fryer basket with olive oil spray.
6. Pat the chicken tenders dry with a paper towel. Dredge the tenders one at a time in the flour, then dip them in the egg, and toss them in the breadcrumb coating. Repeat until all tenders are coated.
7. Set each tender in the air fryer, leaving room on each side of the tender to allow for flipping.
8. When the basket is full, cook 4 to 7 minutes, flip, and cook another 4 to 7 minutes.
9. Remove the tenders and let cool 5 minutes before serving. Repeat until all tenders are cooked.

Sesame Orange Chicken

Servings: 2

Cooking Time: 9 Minutes

Ingredients:

- 1 pound boneless, skinless chicken breasts, cut into cubes
- salt and freshly ground black pepper
- ¼ cup cornstarch
- 2 eggs, beaten
- 1½ cups panko breadcrumbs
- vegetable or peanut oil, in a spray bottle
- 12 ounces orange marmalade
- 1 tablespoon soy sauce
- 1 teaspoon minced ginger
- 2 tablespoons hoisin sauce
- 1 tablespoon sesame oil
- sesame seeds, toasted

Directions:

1. Season the chicken pieces with salt and pepper. Set up a dredging station. Put the cornstarch in a zipper-sealable plastic bag. Place the beaten eggs in a bowl and put the panko breadcrumbs in a shallow dish. Transfer the seasoned chicken to the bag with the cornstarch and shake well to completely coat the chicken on all sides. Remove the chicken from the bag, shaking off any excess cornstarch and dip the pieces into the egg. Let any excess egg drip from the chicken and transfer into the breadcrumbs, pressing the crumbs onto the chicken pieces with your hands. Spray the chicken pieces with vegetable or peanut oil.
2. Preheat the air fryer to 400°F.
3. Combine the orange marmalade, soy sauce, ginger, hoisin sauce and sesame oil in a saucepan. Bring the mixture to a boil on the stovetop, lower the heat and simmer for 10 minutes, until the sauce has thickened. Set aside and keep warm.
4. Transfer the coated chicken to the air fryer basket and air-fry at 400°F for 9 minutes, shaking the basket a few times during the cooking process to help the chicken cook evenly.
5. Right before serving, toss the browned chicken pieces with the sesame orange sauce. Serve over white rice with steamed broccoli. Sprinkle the sesame seeds on top.

Thai Turkey And Zucchini Meatballs

Servings: 4

Cooking Time: 12 Minutes

Ingredients:

- 1½ cups grated zucchini,
- squeezed dry in a clean kitchen towel (about 1 large zucchini)
- 3 scallions, finely chopped
- 2 cloves garlic, minced
- 1 tablespoon grated fresh ginger
- 1 tablespoon finely chopped fresh cilantro
- zest of 1 lime
- 1 teaspoon salt
- freshly ground black pepper
- 1½ pounds ground turkey (a mix of light and dark meat)
- 2 eggs, lightly beaten
- 1 cup Thai sweet chili sauce (spring roll sauce)
- lime wedges, for serving

Directions:

1. Combine the zucchini, scallions, garlic, ginger, cilantro, lime zest, salt, pepper, ground turkey and eggs in a bowl and mix the ingredients together. Gently shape the mixture into 24 balls, about the size of golf balls.
2. Preheat the air fryer to 380°F.
3. Working in batches, air-fry the meatballs for 12 minutes, turning the meatballs over halfway through the cooking time. As soon as the meatballs have finished cooking, toss them in a bowl with the Thai sweet chili sauce to coat.
4. Serve the meatballs over rice noodles or white rice with the remaining Thai sweet chili sauce and lime wedges to squeeze over the top.

Buttermilk-fried Drumsticks

Servings: 2

Cooking Time: 25 Minutes

Ingredients:

- 1 egg
- ½ cup buttermilk
- ¾ cup self-rising flour
- ¾ cup seasoned panko breadcrumbs
- 1 teaspoon salt
- ¼ teaspoon ground black pepper (to mix into coating)
- 4 chicken drumsticks, skin on
- oil for misting or cooking spray

Directions:

1. Beat together egg and buttermilk in shallow dish.
2. In a second shallow dish, combine the flour, panko crumbs, salt, and pepper.
3. Sprinkle chicken legs with additional salt and pepper to taste.
4. Dip legs in buttermilk mixture, then roll in panko mixture, pressing in crumbs to make coating stick. Mist with oil or cooking spray.
5. Spray air fryer basket with cooking spray.
6. Cook drumsticks at 360°F for 10minutes. Turn pieces over and cook an additional 10minutes.
7. Turn pieces to check for browning. If you have any white spots that haven't begun to brown, spritz them with oil or cooking spray. Continue cooking for 5 more minutes or until crust is golden brown and juices run clear. Larger, meatier drumsticks will take longer to cook than small ones.

Chicken Flautas

Servings: 6

Cooking Time: 8 Minutes

Ingredients:

- 6 tablespoons whipped cream cheese
- 1 cup shredded cooked chicken
- 6 tablespoons mild pico de gallo salsa
- ⅓ cup shredded Mexican cheese
- ½ teaspoon taco seasoning
- Six 8-inch flour tortillas
- 2 cups shredded lettuce
- ½ cup guacamole

Directions:

1. Preheat the air fryer to 370°F.
2. In a large bowl, mix the cream cheese, chicken, salsa, shredded cheese, and taco seasoning until well combined.
3. Lay the tortillas on a flat surface. Divide the cheese-and-chicken mixture into 6 equal portions; then place the mixture in the center of the tortillas, spreading evenly, leaving about 1 inch from the edge of the tortilla.
4. Spray the air fryer basket with olive oil spray. Roll up the flautas and place them edge side down into the basket. Lightly mist the top of the flautas with olive oil spray.
5. Repeat until the air fryer basket is full. You may need to cook these in batches, depending on the size of your air fryer.
6. Cook for 7 minutes, or until the outer edges are browned.
7. Remove from the air fryer basket and serve warm over a bed of shredded lettuce with guacamole on top.

Sweet-and-sour Chicken

Servings: 6

Cooking Time: 10 Minutes

Ingredients:

- 1 cup pineapple juice
- 1 cup plus 3 tablespoons cornstarch, divided
- ¼ cup sugar
- ¼ cup ketchup
- ¼ cup apple cider vinegar
- 2 tablespoons soy sauce or tamari
- 1 teaspoon garlic powder, divided
- ¼ cup flour
- 1 tablespoon sesame seeds
- ½ teaspoon salt
- ¼ teaspoon ground black pepper
- 2 large eggs
- 2 pounds chicken breasts, cut into 1-inch cubes
- 1 red bell pepper, cut into 1-inch pieces
- 1 carrot, sliced into ¼-inch-thick rounds

Directions:

1. In a medium saucepan, whisk together the pineapple juice, 3 tablespoons of the cornstarch, the sugar, the ketchup, the apple cider vinegar, the soy sauce or tamari, and ½ teaspoon of the garlic powder. Cook over medium-low heat, whisking occasionally as the sauce thickens, about 6 minutes. Stir and set aside while preparing the chicken.
2. Preheat the air fryer to 370°F.
3. In a medium bowl, place the remaining 1 cup of cornstarch, the flour, the sesame seeds, the salt, the remaining ½ teaspoon of garlic powder, and the pepper.
4. In a second medium bowl, whisk the eggs.
5. Working in batches, place the cubed chicken in the cornstarch mixture to lightly coat; then dip it into the egg mixture, and return it to the cornstarch mixture. Shake off the excess and place the coated chicken in the air fryer basket. Spray with cooking spray and cook for 5 minutes, shake the basket, and spray with more cooking spray. Cook an additional 3 to 5 minutes, or until completely cooked and golden brown.
6. On the last batch of chicken, add the bell pepper and carrot to the basket and cook with the chicken.
7. Place the cooked chicken and vegetables into a serving bowl and toss with the sweet-and-sour sauce to serve.

Air-fried Turkey Breast With Cherry Glaze

Servings: 6

Cooking Time: 54 Minutes

Ingredients:

- 1 (5-pound) turkey breast
- 2 teaspoons olive oil
- 1 teaspoon dried thyme
- ½ teaspoon dried sage
- 1 teaspoon salt
- ½ teaspoon freshly ground black pepper
- ½ cup cherry preserves
- 1 tablespoon chopped fresh thyme leaves
- 1 teaspoon soy sauce*
- freshly ground black pepper

Directions:

1. All turkeys are built differently, so depending on the turkey breast and how your butcher has prepared it, you may need to trim the bottom of the ribs in order to get the turkey to sit upright in the air fryer basket without touching the heating element. The key to this recipe is getting the right size turkey breast. Once you've managed that, the rest is easy, so make sure your turkey breast fits into the air fryer basket before you Preheat the air fryer.
2. Preheat the air fryer to 350°F.
3. Brush the turkey breast all over with the olive oil. Combine the thyme, sage, salt and pepper and rub the outside of the turkey breast with the spice mixture.
4. Transfer the seasoned turkey breast to the air fryer basket, breast side up, and air-fry at 350°F for 25 minutes. Turn the turkey breast on its side and air-fry for another 12 minutes. Turn the turkey breast on the opposite side and air-fry for 12 more minutes. The internal temperature of the turkey breast should reach 165°F when fully cooked.
5. While the turkey is air-frying, make the glaze by combining the cherry preserves, fresh thyme, soy sauce and pepper in a small bowl. When the cooking time is up, return the turkey breast to an upright position and brush the glaze all over the turkey. Air-fry for a final 5 minutes, until the skin is nicely browned and crispy. Let the turkey rest, loosely tented with foil, for at least 5 minutes before slicing and serving.

Spicy Black Bean Turkey Burgers With Cumin-avocado Spread

Servings: 2

Cooking Time: 20 Minutes

Ingredients:

- 1 cup canned black beans, drained and rinsed
- ¾ pound lean ground turkey
- 2 tablespoons minced red onion
- 1 Jalapeño pepper, seeded and minced
- 2 tablespoons plain breadcrumbs
- ½ teaspoon chili powder
- ¼ teaspoon cayenne pepper
- salt, to taste
- olive or vegetable oil
- 2 slices pepper jack cheese
- toasted burger rolls, sliced tomatoes, lettuce leaves
- Cumin-Avocado Spread:
- 1 ripe avocado
- juice of 1 lime
- 1 teaspoon ground cumin
- ½ teaspoon salt
- 1 tablespoon chopped fresh cilantro
- freshly ground black pepper

Directions:

1. Place the black beans in a large bowl and smash them slightly with the back of a fork. Add the ground turkey, red onion, Jalapeño pepper, breadcrumbs, chili powder and cayenne pepper. Season with salt. Mix with your hands to combine all the ingredients and then shape them into 2 patties. Brush both sides of the burger patties with a little olive or vegetable oil.
2. Preheat the air fryer to 380°F.
3. Transfer the burgers to the air fryer basket and air-fry for 20 minutes, flipping them over halfway through the cooking process. Top the burgers with the pepper jack cheese (securing the slices to the burgers with a toothpick) for the last 2 minutes of the cooking process.
4. While the burgers are cooking, make the cumin avocado spread. Place the avocado, lime juice, cumin and salt in food processor and process until smooth. (For a chunkier spread, you can mash this by hand in a bowl.) Stir in the cilantro and season with freshly ground black pepper. Chill the spread until you are ready to serve.
5. When the burgers have finished cooking, remove them from the air fryer and let them rest on a plate, covered gently with aluminum foil. Brush a little olive oil on the insides of the burger rolls. Place the rolls, cut side up, into the air fryer basket and air-fry at 400°F for 1 minute to toast and warm them.
6. Spread the cumin-avocado spread on the rolls and build your burgers with lettuce and sliced tomatoes and any other ingredient you like. Serve warm with a side of sweet potato fries.

Apricot Glazed Chicken Thighs

Servings: 2

Cooking Time: 22 Minutes

Ingredients:

- 4 bone-in chicken thighs (about 2 pounds)
- olive oil
- 1 teaspoon salt
- ¼ teaspoon freshly ground black pepper
- ½ teaspoon onion powder
- ¾ cup apricot preserves 1½ tablespoons Dijon mustard
- ½ teaspoon dried thyme
- 1 teaspoon soy sauce
- fresh thyme leaves, for garnish

Directions:

1. Preheat the air fryer to 380°F.
2. Brush or spray both the air fryer basket and the chicken with the olive oil. Combine the salt, pepper and onion powder and season both sides of the chicken with the spice mixture.
3. Place the seasoned chicken thighs, skin side down in the air fryer basket. Air-fry for 10 minutes.
4. While chicken is cooking, make the glaze by combining the apricot preserves, Dijon mustard, thyme and soy sauce in a small bowl.
5. When the time is up on the air fryer, spoon half of the apricot glaze over the chicken thighs and air-fry for 2 minutes. Then flip the chicken thighs over so that the skin side is facing up and air-fry for an additional 8 minutes. Finally, spoon and spread the rest of the glaze evenly over the chicken thighs and air-fry for a final 2 minutes. Transfer the chicken to a serving platter and sprinkle the fresh thyme leaves on top.

VEGETABLE SIDE DISHES RECIPES

Grits Again

Servings: 2

Cooking Time: 10 Minutes

Ingredients:

- cooked grits
- plain breadcrumbs
- oil for misting or cooking spray
- honey or maple syrup for serving (optional)

Directions:

1. While grits are still warm, spread them into a square or rectangular baking pan, about ½-inch thick. If your grits are thicker than that, scoop some out into another pan.
2. Chill several hours or overnight, until grits are cold and firm.
3. When ready to cook, pour off any water that has collected in pan and cut grits into 2- to 3-inch squares.
4. Dip grits squares in breadcrumbs and place in air fryer basket in single layer, close but not touching.
5. Cook at 390°F for 10 minutes, until heated through and crispy brown on the outside.
6. Serve while hot either plain or with a drizzle of honey or maple syrup.

Cheesy Potato Skins

Servings: 6

Cooking Time: 54 Minutes

Ingredients:

- 3 6- to 8-ounce small russet potatoes
- 3 Thick-cut bacon strips, halved widthwise (gluten-free, if a concern)
- ¾ teaspoon Mild paprika
- ¼ teaspoon Garlic powder
- ¼ teaspoon Table salt
- ¼ teaspoon Ground black pepper
- ½ cup plus 1 tablespoon (a little over 2 ounces) Shredded Cheddar cheese
- 3 tablespoons Thinly sliced trimmed chives
- 6 tablespoons (a little over 1 ounce) Finely grated Parmesan cheese

Directions:

1. Preheat the air fryer to 375°F .
2. Prick each potato in four places with a fork (not four places in a line but four places all around the potato). Set the potatoes in the basket with as much air space between them as possible. Air-fry undisturbed for 45 minutes, or until the potatoes are tender when pricked with a fork.
3. Use kitchen tongs to gently transfer the potatoes to a wire rack. Cool for 15 minutes. Maintain the machine's temperature.
4. Lay the bacon strip halves in the basket in one layer. They may touch but should not overlap. Air-fry undisturbed for 5 minutes, until crisp. Use those same tongs to transfer the bacon pieces to the wire rack. If there's a great deal of rendered bacon fat in the basket's bottom or on a tray under the basket attachment, pour this into a bowl, cool, and discard. Don't throw it down the drain!
5. Cut the potatoes in half lengthwise (not just slit them open but actually cut in half). Use a flatware spoon to scoop the hot, soft middles into a bowl, leaving ½ inch of potato all around the inside of the spud next to the skin. Sprinkle the inside of the potato "shells" evenly with paprika, garlic powder, salt, and pepper.
6. Chop the bacon pieces into small bits. Sprinkle these along with the Cheddar and chives evenly inside the potato shells. Crumble 2 to 3 tablespoons of the soft potato insides over the filling mixture. Divide the grated Parmesan evenly over the tops of the potatoes.
7. Set the stuffed potatoes in the basket with as much air space between them as possible. Air-fry undisturbed for 4 minutes, until the cheese melts and lightly browns.
8. Use kitchen tongs to gently transfer the stuffed potato halves to a wire rack. Cool for 5 minutes before serving.

Homemade Potato Puffs

Servings: 4

Cooking Time: 15 Minutes

Ingredients:

- 1¾ cups Water
- 4 tablespoons (¼ cup/½ stick) Butter
- 2 cups plus 2 tablespoons Instant mashed potato flakes
- 1½ teaspoons Table salt
- ¾ teaspoon Ground black pepper
- ¼ teaspoon Mild paprika
- ¼ teaspoon Dried thyme
- 1¼ cups Seasoned Italian-style dried bread crumbs (gluten-free, if a concern)
- Olive oil spray

Directions:

1. Heat the water with the butter in a medium saucepan set over medium-low heat just until the butter melts. Do not bring to a boil.
2. Remove the saucepan from the heat and stir in the potato flakes, salt, pepper, paprika, and thyme until smooth. Set aside to cool for 5 minutes.
3. Preheat the air fryer to 400°F. Spread the bread crumbs on a dinner plate.
4. Scrape up 2 tablespoons of the potato flake mixture and form it into a small, oblong puff, like a little cylinder about 1½ inches long. Gently roll the puff in the bread crumbs until coated on all sides. Set it aside and continue making more, about 12 for the small batch, 18 for the medium batch, or 24 for the large.
5. Coat the potato cylinders with olive oil spray on all sides, then arrange them in the basket in one layer with some air space between them. Air-fry undisturbed for 15 minutes, or until crisp and brown.
6. Gently dump the contents of the basket onto a wire rack. Cool for 5 minutes before serving.

Hasselback Garlic-and-butter Potatoes

Servings: 3

Cooking Time: 48 Minutes

Ingredients:

- 3 8-ounce russet potatoes
- 6 Brown button or Baby Bella mushrooms, very thinly sliced
- Olive oil spray
- 3 tablespoons Butter, melted and cooled
- 1 tablespoon Minced garlic
- ¾ teaspoon Table salt
- 3 tablespoons (about ½ ounce) Finely grated Parmesan cheese

Directions:

1. Preheat the air fryer to 350°F .
2. Cut slits down the length of each potato, about three-quarters down into the potato and spaced about ¼ inch apart. Wedge a thin mushroom slice in each slit. Generously coat the potatoes on all sides with olive oil spray.
3. When the machine is at temperature, set the potatoes mushroom side up in the basket with as much air space between them as possible. Air-fry undisturbed for 45 minutes, or tender when pricked with a fork.
4. Increase the machine's temperature to 400°F. Use kitchen tongs, and perhaps a flatware fork for balance, to gently transfer the potatoes to a cutting board. Brush each evenly with butter, then sprinkle the minced garlic and salt over them. Sprinkle the cheese evenly over the potatoes.
5. Use those same tongs to gently transfer the potatoes cheese side up to the basket in one layer with some space for air flow between them. Air-fry undisturbed for 3 minutes, or until the cheese has melted and begun to brown.
6. Use those same tongs to gently transfer the potatoes back to the wire rack. Cool for 5 minutes before serving.

Onions

Servings: 4

Cooking Time: 18 Minutes

Ingredients:

- 2 yellow onions (Vidalia or 1015 recommended)
- salt and pepper
- ¼ teaspoon ground thyme
- ¼ teaspoon smoked paprika
- 2 teaspoons olive oil
- 1 ounce Gruyère cheese, grated

Directions:

1. Peel onions and halve lengthwise (vertically).
2. Sprinkle cut sides of onions with salt, pepper, thyme, and paprika.
3. Place each onion half, cut-surface up, on a large square of aluminum foil. Pull sides of foil up to cup around onion. Drizzle cut surface of onions with oil.
4. Crimp foil at top to seal closed.
5. Place wrapped onions in air fryer basket and cook at 390°F for 18 minutes. When done, onions should be soft enough to pierce with fork but still slightly firm.
6. Open foil just enough to sprinkle each onion with grated cheese.
7. Cook for 30 seconds to 1 minute to melt cheese.

Roasted Eggplant Halves With Herbed Ricotta

Servings: 3

Cooking Time: 20 Minutes

Ingredients:

- 3 5- to 6-ounce small eggplants, stemmed
- Olive oil spray
- ¼ teaspoon Table salt
- ¼ teaspoon Ground black pepper
- ½ cup Regular or low-fat ricotta
- 1½ tablespoons Minced fresh basil leaves
- 1¼ teaspoons Minced fresh oregano leaves
- Honey

Directions:

1. Preheat the air fryer to 325°F (or 330°F, if that's the closest setting).
2. Cut the eggplants in half lengthwise. Set them cut side up on your work surface. Using the tip of a paring knife, make a series of slits about three-quarters down into the flesh of each eggplant half; work at a 45-degree angle to the (former) stem across the vegetable and make the slits about ½ inch apart. Make a second set of equidistant slits at a 90-degree angle to the first slits, thus creating a crosshatch pattern in the vegetable.
3. Generously coat the cut sides of the eggplants with olive oil spray. Sprinkle the salt and pepper over the cut surfaces.
4. Set the eggplant halves cut side up in the basket with as much air space between them as possible. Air-fry undisturbed for 20 minutes, or until soft and golden.
5. Use kitchen tongs to gently transfer the eggplant halves to serving plates or a platter. Cool for 5 minutes.
6. Whisk the ricotta, basil, and oregano in a small bowl until well combined. Top the eggplant halves with this mixture. Drizzle the halves with honey to taste before serving warm.

Moroccan-spiced Carrots

Servings: 4

Cooking Time: 30 Minutes

Ingredients:

- 1¼ pounds Baby carrots
- 2 tablespoons Butter, melted and cooled
- 1 teaspoon Mild smoked paprika
- 1 teaspoon Ground cumin
- ¾ teaspoon Ground coriander
- ¾ teaspoon Ground dried ginger
- ¼ teaspoon Ground cinnamon
- ½ teaspoon Table salt
- ¼ teaspoon Ground black pepper

Directions:

1. Preheat the air fryer to 400°F.
2. Toss the carrots, melted butter, smoked paprika, cumin, coriander, ginger, cinnamon, salt, and pepper in a large bowl until the carrots are evenly and thoroughly coated.
3. When the machine is at temperature, scrape the carrots into the basket, spreading them into as close to one layer as you can. Air-fry for 30 minutes, tossing and rearranging the carrots every 8 minutes (that is, three times), until crisp-tender and lightly browned in spots.
4. Pour the contents of the basket into a serving bowl or platter. Cool for a couple of minutes, then serve warm or at room temperature.

Asparagus Fries

Servings: 4

Cooking Time: 5 Minutes Per Batch

Ingredients:

- 12 ounces fresh asparagus spears with tough ends trimmed off
- 2 egg whites
- ¼ cup water
- ¾ cup panko breadcrumbs
- ¼ cup grated Parmesan cheese, plus 2 tablespoons
- ¼ teaspoon salt
- oil for misting or cooking spray

Directions:

1. Preheat air fryer to 390°F.
2. In a shallow dish, beat egg whites and water until slightly foamy.
3. In another shallow dish, combine panko, Parmesan, and salt.
4. Dip asparagus spears in egg, then roll in crumbs. Spray with oil or cooking spray.
5. Place a layer of asparagus in air fryer basket, leaving just a little space in between each spear. Stack another layer on top, crosswise. Cook at 390°F for 5 minutes, until crispy and golden brown.
6. Repeat to cook remaining asparagus.

Fried Eggplant Balls

Servings: 4 Cooking Time: 40 Minutes

Ingredients:

- 1 medium eggplant (about 1 pound)
- olive oil
- salt and freshly ground black pepper
- 1 cup grated Parmesan cheese
- 2 cups fresh breadcrumbs
- 2 tablespoons chopped fresh parsley
- 2 tablespoons chopped fresh basil
- 1 clove garlic, minced
- 1 egg, lightly beaten
- ½ cup fine dried breadcrumbs

Directions:

1. Preheat the air fryer to 400°F.
2. Quarter the eggplant by cutting it in half both lengthwise and horizontally. Make a few slashes in the flesh of the eggplant but not through the skin. Brush the cut surface of the eggplant generously with olive oil and transfer to the air fryer basket, cut side up. Air-fry for 10 minutes. Turn the eggplant quarters cut side down and air-fry for another 15 minutes or until the eggplant is soft all the way through. You may need to rotate the pieces in the air fryer so that they cook evenly. Transfer the eggplant to a cutting board to cool.
3. Place the Parmesan cheese, the fresh breadcrumbs, fresh herbs, garlic and egg in a food processor. Scoop the flesh out of the eggplant, discarding the skin and any pieces that are tough. You should have about 1 to 1½ cups of eggplant. Add the eggplant to the food processor and process everything together until smooth. Season with salt and pepper. Refrigerate the mixture for at least 30 minutes.
4. Place the dried breadcrumbs into a shallow dish or onto a plate. Scoop heaping tablespoons of the eggplant mixture into the dried breadcrumbs. Roll the dollops of eggplant in the breadcrumbs and then shape into small balls. You should have 16 to 18 eggplant balls at the end. Refrigerate until you are ready to air-fry.
5. Preheat the air fryer to 350°F.
6. Spray the eggplant balls and the air fryer basket with olive oil. Air-fry the eggplant balls for 15 minutes, rotating the balls during the cooking process to brown evenly.

Zucchini Fries

Servings: 3

Cooking Time: 12 Minutes

Ingredients:

- 1 large Zucchini
- ½ cup All-purpose flour or tapioca flour
- 2 Large egg(s), well beaten
- 1 cup Seasoned Italian-style dried bread crumbs (gluten-free, if a concern)
- Olive oil spray

Directions:

1. Preheat the air fryer to 400°F.
2. Trim the zucchini into a long rectangular block, taking off the ends and four "sides" to make this shape. Cut the block lengthwise into ½-inch-thick slices. Lay these slices flat and cut in half widthwise. Slice each of these pieces into ½-inch-thick batons.
3. Set up and fill three shallow soup plates or small pie plates on your counter: one for the flour, one for the beaten egg(s), and one for the bread crumbs.
4. Set a zucchini baton in the flour and turn it several times to coat all sides. Gently shake off any excess flour, then dip it in the egg(s), turning it to coat. Let any excess egg slip back into the rest, then set the baton in the bread crumbs and turn it several times, pressing gently to coat all sides, even the ends. Set aside on a cutting board and continue coating the remainder of the batons in the same way.
5. Lightly coat the batons on all sides with olive oil spray. Set them in two flat layers in the basket, the top layer at a 90-degree angle to the bottom one, with a little air space between the batons in each layer. In the end, the whole thing will look like a crosshatch pattern. Air-fry undisturbed for 6 minutes.
6. Use kitchen tongs to gently rearrange the batons so that any covered parts are now uncovered. The batons no longer need to be in a crosshatch pattern. Continue air-frying undisturbed for 6 minutes, or until lightly browned and crisp.
7. Gently pour the contents of the basket onto a wire rack. Spread the batons out and cool for only a minute or two before serving.

Roasted Fennel Salad

Servings: 3

Cooking Time: 20 Minutes

Ingredients:

- 3 cups (about ¾ pound) Trimmed fennel (see the headnote), roughly chopped
- 1½ tablespoons Olive oil
- ¼ teaspoon Table salt
- ¼ teaspoon Ground black pepper
- 1½ tablespoons White balsamic vinegar (see here)

Directions:

1. Preheat the air fryer to 400°F.
2. Toss the fennel, olive oil, salt, and pepper in a large bowl until the fennel is well coated in the oil.
3. When the machine is at temperature, pour the fennel into the basket, spreading it out into as close to one layer as possible. Air-fry for 20 minutes, tossing and rearranging the fennel pieces twice so that any covered or touching parts get exposed to the air currents, until golden at the edges and softened.
4. Pour the fennel into a serving bowl. Add the vinegar while hot. Toss well, then cool a couple of minutes before serving. Or serve at room temperature.

Brown Rice And Goat Cheese Croquettes

Servings: 3

Cooking Time: 8 Minutes

Ingredients:

- ¾ cup Water
- 6 tablespoons Raw medium-grain brown rice, such as brown Arborio
- ½ cup Shredded carrot
- ¼ cup Walnut pieces
- 3 tablespoons (about 1½ ounces) Soft goat cheese
- 1 tablespoon Pasteurized egg substitute, such as Egg Beaters (gluten-free, if a concern)
- ¼ teaspoon Dried thyme
- ¼ teaspoon Table salt
- ¼ teaspoon Ground black pepper
- Olive oil spray

Directions:

1. Combine the water, rice, and carrots in a small saucepan set over medium-high heat. Bring to a boil, stirring occasionally. Cover, reduce the heat to very low, and simmer very slowly for 45 minutes, or until the water has been absorbed and the rice is tender. Set aside, covered, for 10 minutes.
2. Scrape the contents of the saucepan into a food processor. Cool for 10 minutes.
3. Preheat the air fryer to 400°F.
4. Put the nuts, cheese, egg substitute, thyme, salt, and pepper into the food processor. Cover and pulse to a coarse paste, stopping the machine at least once to scrape down the inside of the canister.
5. Uncover the food processor; scrape down and remove the blade. Using wet, clean hands, form the mixture into two 4-inch-diameter patties for a small batch, three 4-inch-diameter patties for a medium batch, or four 4-inch-diameter patties for a large one. Generously coat both sides of the patties with olive oil spray.
6. Set the patties in the basket with as much air space between them as possible. Air-fry undisturbed for 8 minutes, or until brown and crisp.
7. Use a nonstick-safe spatula to transfer the croquettes to a wire rack. Cool for 5 minutes before serving.

DESSERTS AND SWEETS

Fried Oreos

Servings: 12

Cooking Time: 6 Minutes Per Batch

Ingredients:

- oil for misting or nonstick spray
- 1 cup complete pancake and waffle mix
- 1 teaspoon vanilla extract
- ½ cup water, plus 2 tablespoons
- 12 Oreos or other chocolate sandwich cookies
- 1 tablespoon confectioners' sugar

Directions:

1. Spray baking pan with oil or nonstick spray and place in basket.
2. Preheat air fryer to 390°F.
3. In a medium bowl, mix together the pancake mix, vanilla, and water.
4. Dip 4 cookies in batter and place in baking pan.
5. Cook for 6minutes, until browned.
6. Repeat steps 4 and 5 for the remaining cookies.
7. Sift sugar over warm cookies.

Banana Bread Cake

Servings: 6

Cooking Time: 18-22 Minutes

Ingredients:

- ¾ cup plus 2 tablespoons All-purpose flour
- ½ teaspoon Baking powder
- ¼ teaspoon Baking soda
- ¼ teaspoon Table salt
- 4 tablespoons (¼ cup/½ stick) Butter, at room temperature
- ½ cup Granulated white sugar
- 2 Small ripe bananas, peeled
- 5 tablespoons Pasteurized egg substitute, such as Egg Beaters
- ¼ cup Buttermilk
- ¾ teaspoon Vanilla extract
- Baking spray (see here)

Directions:

1. Preheat the air fryer to 325°F (or 330°F, if that's the closest setting).
2. Mix the flour, baking powder, baking soda, and salt in a small bowl until well combined.
3. Using an electric hand mixer at medium speed, beat the butter and sugar in a medium bowl until creamy and smooth, about 3 minutes, occasionally scraping down the inside of the bowl.
4. Beat in the bananas until smooth. Then beat in egg substitute or egg, buttermilk, and vanilla until uniform. (The batter may look curdled at this stage. The flour mixture will smooth it out.) Add the flour mixture and beat at low speed until smooth and creamy.
5. Use the baking spray to generously coat the inside of a 6-inch round cake pan for a small batch, a 7-inch round cake pan for a medium batch, or an 8-inch round cake pan for a large batch. Scrape and spread the batter into the pan, smoothing the batter out to an even layer.
6. Set the pan in the basket and air-fry for 18 minutes for a 6-inch layer, 20 minutes for a 7-inch layer, or 22 minutes for an 8-inch layer, or until the cake is well browned and set even if there's a little soft give right at the center. Start checking it at the 16-minute mark to know where you are.
7. Use hot pads or silicone baking mitts to transfer the cake pan to a wire rack. To unmold, set a cutting board over the baking pan and invert both the board and the pan. Lift the still-warm pan off the cake layer. Set the wire rack on top of that layer and invert all of it with the cutting board so that the cake layer is now right side up on the wire rack. Remove the cutting board and continue cooling the cake for at least 10 minutes or to room temperature, about 40 minutes, before slicing into wedges.

Pear And Almond Biscotti Crumble

Servings: 6

Cooking Time: 65 Minutes

Ingredients:

- 7-inch cake pan or ceramic dish
- 3 pears, peeled, cored and sliced
- ½ cup brown sugar
- ¼ teaspoon ground ginger
- 1 teaspoon ground cinnamon
- ⅛ teaspoon ground nutmeg
- 2 tablespoons cornstarch
- 1¼ cups (4 to 5) almond biscotti, coarsely crushed
- ¼ cup all-purpose flour
- ¼ cup sliced almonds
- ¼ cup butter, melted

Directions:

1. Combine the pears, brown sugar, ginger, cinnamon, nutmeg and cornstarch in a bowl. Toss to combine and then pour the pear mixture into a greased 7-inch cake pan or ceramic dish.
2. Combine the crushed biscotti, flour, almonds and melted butter in a medium bowl. Toss with a fork until the mixture resembles large crumbles. Sprinkle the biscotti crumble over the pears and cover the pan with aluminum foil.
3. Preheat the air fryer to 350°F.
4. Air-fry at 350°F for 60 minutes. Remove the aluminum foil and air-fry for an additional 5 minutes to brown the crumble layer.
5. Serve warm.

Fudgy Brownie Cake

Servings: 6

Cooking Time: 25-35 Minutes

Ingredients:

- 6½ tablespoons All-purpose flour
- ¼ cup plus 1 teaspoon Unsweetened cocoa powder
- ½ teaspoon Baking powder
- ¼ teaspoon Table salt
- 6½ tablespoons Butter, at room temperature
- 9½ tablespoons Granulated white sugar
- 1 egg plus 1 large egg white Large egg(s)
- ¾ teaspoon Vanilla extract
- Baking spray (see here)

Directions:

1. Preheat the air fryer to 325°F (or 330°F, if that's the closest setting).
2. Mix the flour, cocoa powder, baking powder, and salt in a small bowl until well combined.
3. Using an electric hand mixer at medium speed, beat the butter and sugar in a medium bowl until creamy and smooth, about 3 minutes, occasionally scraping down the inside of the bowl.
4. Beat in the egg(s) and the white or yolk (as necessary), as well as the vanilla, until smooth. Turn off the beaters and add the flour mixture. Beat at low speed until thick and smooth.
5. Use the baking spray to generously coat the inside of a 6-inch round cake pan for a small batch, a 7-inch round cake pan for a medium batch, or an 8-inch round cake pan for a large batch. Scrape and spread the batter into the pan, smoothing the batter out to an even layer.
6. Set the pan in the basket and air-fry for 25 minutes for a 6-inch layer, 30 minutes for a 7-inch layer, or 35 minutes for an 8-inch layer, or until the cake is set but soft to the touch. Start checking it at the 20-minute mark to know where you are.
7. Use hot pads or silicone baking mitts to transfer the cake pan to a wire rack. Cool for at least 1 hour or up to 4 hours. Using a nonstick-safe knife, slice the cake into wedges right in the pan and lift them out one by one.

Giant Oatmeal–peanut Butter Cookie

Servings: 4

Cooking Time: 18 Minutes

Ingredients:

- 1 cup Rolled oats (not quick-cooking or steel-cut oats)
- ½ cup All-purpose flour
- ½ teaspoon Ground cinnamon
- ½ teaspoon Baking soda
- ⅓ cup Packed light brown sugar
- ¼ cup Solid vegetable shortening
- 2 tablespoons Natural-style creamy peanut butter
- 3 tablespoons Granulated white sugar
- 2 tablespoons (or 1 small egg, well beaten) Pasteurized egg substitute, such as Egg Beaters
- ⅓ cup Roasted, salted peanuts, chopped
- Baking spray

Directions:

1. Preheat the air fryer to 350°F .
2. Stir the oats, flour, cinnamon, and baking soda in a bowl until well combined.
3. Using an electric hand mixer at medium speed, beat the brown sugar, shortening, peanut butter, granulated white sugar, and egg substitute or egg (as applicable) until smooth and creamy, about 3 minutes, scraping down the inside of the bowl occasionally.
4. Scrape down and remove the beaters. Fold in the flour mixture and peanuts with a rubber spatula just until all the flour is moistened and the peanut bits are evenly distributed in the dough.
5. For a small air fryer, coat the inside of a 6-inch round cake pan with baking spray. For a medium air fryer, coat the inside of a 7-inch round cake pan with baking spray. And for a large air fryer, coat the inside of an 8-inch round cake pan with baking spray. Scrape and gently press the dough into the prepared pan, spreading it into an even layer to the perimeter.
6. Set the pan in the basket and air-fry undisturbed for 18 minutes, or until well browned.
7. Transfer the pan to a wire rack and cool for 15 minutes. Loosen the cookie from the perimeter with a spatula, then invert the pan onto a cutting board and let the cookie come free. Remove the pan and reinvert the cookie onto the wire rack. Cool for 5 minutes more before slicing into wedges to serve.

Giant Vegan Chocolate Chip Cookie

Servings: 4

Cooking Time: 16 Minutes

Ingredients:

- ⅔ cup All-purpose flour
- 5 tablespoons Rolled oats (not quick-cooking or steel-cut oats)
- ¼ teaspoon Baking soda
- ¼ teaspoon Table salt
- 5 tablespoons Granulated white sugar
- ¼ cup Vegetable oil
- 2½ tablespoons Tahini (see here)
- 2½ tablespoons Maple syrup
- 2 teaspoons Vanilla extract
- ⅔ cup Vegan semisweet or bittersweet chocolate chips
- Baking spray

Directions:

1. Preheat the air fryer to 325°F (or 330°F, if that's the closest setting).
2. Whisk the flour, oats, baking soda, and salt in a bowl until well combined.
3. Using an electric hand mixer at medium speed, beat the sugar, oil, tahini, maple syrup, and vanilla until rich and creamy, about 3 minutes, scraping down the inside of the bowl occasionally.
4. Scrape down and remove the beaters. Fold in the flour mixture and chocolate chips with a rubber spatula just until all the flour is moistened and the chocolate chips are even throughout the dough.
5. For a small air fryer, coat the inside of a 6-inch round cake pan with baking spray. For a medium air fryer, coat the inside of a 7-inch round cake pan with baking spray. And for a large air fryer, coat the inside of an 8-inch round cake pan with baking spray. Scrape and gently press the dough into the prepared pan, spreading it into an even layer to the perimeter.
6. Set the pan in the basket and air-fry undisturbed for 16 minutes, or until puffed, browned, and firm to the touch.
7. Transfer the pan to a wire rack and cool for 10 minutes. Loosen the cookie from the perimeter with a spatula, then invert the pan onto a cutting board and let the cookie come free. Remove the pan and reinvert the cookie onto the wire rack. Cool for 5 minutes more before slicing into wedges to serve.

Baked Apple

Servings: 6

Cooking Time: 20 Minutes

Ingredients:

- 3 small Honey Crisp or other baking apples
- 3 tablespoons maple syrup
- 3 tablespoons chopped pecans
- 1 tablespoon firm butter, cut into 6 pieces

Directions:

1. Put ½ cup water in the drawer of the air fryer.
2. Wash apples well and dry them.
3. Split apples in half. Remove core and a little of the flesh to make a cavity for the pecans.
4. Place apple halves in air fryer basket, cut side up.
5. Spoon 1½ teaspoons pecans into each cavity.
6. Spoon ½ tablespoon maple syrup over pecans in each apple.
7. Top each apple with ½ teaspoon butter.
8. Cook at 360°F for 20 minutes, until apples are tender.

Chocolate Macaroons

Servings: 16

Cooking Time: 8 Minutes

Ingredients:

- 2 Large egg white(s), at room temperature
- ⅛ teaspoon Table salt
- ½ cup Granulated white sugar
- 1½ cups Unsweetened shredded coconut
- 3 tablespoons Unsweetened cocoa powder

Directions:

1. Preheat the air fryer to 375°F .
2. Using an electric mixer at high speed, beat the egg white(s) and salt in a medium or large bowl until stiff peaks can be formed when the turned-off beaters are dipped into the mixture.
3. Still working with the mixer at high speed, beat in the sugar in a slow stream until the meringue is shiny and thick.
4. Scrape down and remove the beaters. Fold in the coconut and cocoa with a rubber spatula until well combined, working carefully to deflate the meringue as little as possible.
5. Scoop up 2 tablespoons of the mixture. Wet your clean hands and roll that little bit of coconut bliss into a ball. Set it aside and continue making more balls: 7 more for a small batch, 15 more for a medium batch, or 23 more for a large one.
6. Line the bottom of the machine's basket or the basket attachment with parchment paper. Set the balls on the parchment with as much air space between them as possible. Air-fry undisturbed for 8 minutes, or until dry, set, and lightly browned.
7. Use a nonstick-safe spatula to transfer the macaroons to a wire rack. Cool for at least 10 minutes before serving. Or cool to room temperature, about 30 minutes, then store in a sealed container at room temperature for up to 3 days.

Blueberry Crisp

Servings: 6

Cooking Time: 13 Minutes

Ingredients:

- 3 cups Fresh or thawed frozen blueberries
- ⅓ cup Granulated white sugar
- 1 tablespoon Instant tapioca
- ⅓ cup All-purpose flour
- ⅓ cup Rolled oats (not quick-cooking or steel-cut)
- ⅓ cup Chopped walnuts or pecans
- ⅓ cup Packed light brown sugar
- 5 tablespoons plus 1 teaspoon (⅔ stick) Butter, melted and cooled
- ¾ teaspoon Ground cinnamon
- ¼ teaspoon Table salt

Directions:

1. Preheat the air fryer to 400°F.
2. Mix the blueberries, granulated white sugar, and instant tapioca in a 6-inch round cake pan for a small batch, a 7-inch round cake pan for a medium batch, or an 8-inch round cake pan for a large batch.
3. When the machine is at temperature, set the cake pan in the basket and air-fry undisturbed for 5 minutes, or just until the blueberries begin to bubble.
4. Meanwhile, mix the flour, oats, nuts, brown sugar, butter, cinnamon, and salt in a medium bowl until well combined.
5. When the blueberries have begun to bubble, crumble this flour mixture evenly on top. Continue air-frying undisturbed for 8 minutes, or until the topping has browned a bit and the filling is bubbling.
6. Use two hot pads or silicone baking mitts to transfer the cake pan to a wire rack. Cool for at least 10 minutes or to room temperature before serving.

Boston Cream Donut Holes

Servings: 24

Cooking Time: 12 Minutes

Ingredients:

- 1½ cups bread flour
- 1 teaspoon active dry yeast
- 1 tablespoon sugar
- ¼ teaspoon salt
- ½ cup warm milk
- ½ teaspoon pure vanilla extract
- 2 egg yolks
- 2 tablespoons butter, melted
- vegetable oil
- Custard Filling:
- 1 (3.4-ounce) box French vanilla instant pudding mix
- ¾ cup whole milk
- ¼ cup heavy cream
- Chocolate Glaze:
- 1 cup chocolate chips
- ⅓ cup heavy cream

Directions:

1. Combine the flour, yeast, sugar and salt in the bowl of a stand mixer. Add the milk, vanilla, egg yolks and butter. Mix until the dough starts to come together in a ball. Transfer the dough to a floured surface and knead the dough by hand for 2 minutes. Shape the dough into a ball, place it in a large oiled bowl, cover the bowl with a clean kitchen towel and let the dough rise for 1 to 1½ hours or until the dough has doubled in size.
2. When the dough has risen, punch it down and roll it into a 24-inch log. Cut the dough into 24 pieces and roll each piece into a ball. Place the dough balls on a baking sheet and let them rise for another 30 minutes.
3. Preheat the air fryer to 400°F.
4. Spray or brush the dough balls lightly with vegetable oil and air-fry eight at a time for 4 minutes, turning them over halfway through the cooking time.
5. While donut holes are cooking, make the filling and chocolate glaze. To make the filling, use an electric hand mixer to beat the French vanilla pudding, milk and ¼ cup of heavy cream together for 2 minutes.
6. To make the chocolate glaze, place the chocolate chips in a medium-sized bowl. Bring the heavy cream to a boil on the stovetop and pour it over the chocolate chips. Stir until the chips are melted and the glaze is smooth.
7. To fill the donut holes, place the custard filling in a pastry bag with a long tip. Poke a hole into the side of the donut hole with a small knife. Wiggle the knife around to make room for the filling. Place the pastry bag tip into the hole and slowly squeeze the custard into the center of the donut. Dip the top half of the donut into the chocolate glaze, letting any excess glaze drip back into the bowl. Let the glazed donut holes sit for a few minutes before serving.

Fried Cannoli Wontons

Servings: 10

Cooking Time: 8 Minutes

Ingredients:

- 8 ounces Neufchâtel cream cheese
- ¼ cup powdered sugar
- 1 teaspoon vanilla extract
- ¼ teaspoon salt
- ¼ cup mini chocolate chips
- 2 tablespoons chopped pecans (optional)
- 20 wonton wrappers
- ¼ cup filtered water

Directions:

1. Preheat the air fryer to 370°F.
2. In a large bowl, use a hand mixer to combine the cream cheese with the powdered sugar, vanilla, and salt. Fold in the chocolate chips and pecans. Set aside.
3. Lay the wonton wrappers out on a flat, smooth surface and place a bowl with the filtered water next to them.
4. Use a teaspoon to evenly divide the cream cheese mixture among the 20 wonton wrappers, placing the batter in the center of the wontons.
5. Wet the tip of your index finger, and gently moisten the outer edges of the wrapper. Then fold each wrapper until it creates a secure pocket.
6. Liberally spray the air fryer basket with olive oil mist.
7. Place the wontons into the basket, and cook for 5 to 8 minutes. When the outer edges begin to brown, remove the wontons from the air fryer basket. Repeat cooking with remaining wontons.
8. Serve warm.

Honey-roasted Mixed Nuts

Servings: 8

Cooking Time: 15 Minutes

Ingredients:

- ½ cup raw, shelled pistachios
- ½ cup raw almonds
- 1 cup raw walnuts
- 2 tablespoons filtered water
- 2 tablespoons honey
- 1 tablespoon vegetable oil
- 2 tablespoons sugar
- ½ teaspoon salt

Directions:

1. Preheat the air fryer to 300°F.
2. Lightly spray an air-fryer-safe pan with olive oil; then place the pistachios, almonds, and walnuts inside the pan and place the pan inside the air fryer basket.
3. Cook for 15 minutes, shaking the basket every 5 minutes to rotate the nuts.
4. While the nuts are roasting, boil the water in a small pan and stir in the honey and oil. Continue to stir while cooking until the water begins to evaporate and a thick sauce is formed. Note: The sauce should stick to the back of a wooden spoon when mixed. Turn off the heat.
5. Remove the nuts from the air fryer (cooking should have just completed) and spoon the nuts into the stovetop pan. Use a spatula to coat the nuts with the honey syrup.
6. Line a baking sheet with parchment paper and spoon the nuts onto the sheet. Lightly sprinkle the sugar and salt over the nuts and let cool in the refrigerator for at least 2 hours.
7. When the honey and sugar have hardened, store the nuts in an airtight container in the refrigerator.

BREAD AND BREAKFAST

Scones

Servings: 9

Cooking Time: 8 Minutes Per Batch

Ingredients:

- 2 cups self-rising flour, plus ¼ cup for kneading
- ⅓ cup granulated sugar
- ¼ cup butter, cold
- 1 cup milk

Directions:

1. Preheat air fryer at 360°F.
2. In large bowl, stir together flour and sugar.
3. Cut cold butter into tiny cubes, and stir into flour mixture with fork.
4. Stir in milk until soft dough forms.
5. Sprinkle ¼ cup of flour onto wax paper and place dough on top. Knead lightly by folding and turning the dough about 6 to 8 times.
6. Pat dough into a 6 x 6-inch square.
7. Cut into 9 equal squares.
8. Place all squares in air fryer basket or as many as will fit in a single layer, close together but not touching.
9. Cook at 360°F for 8minutes. When done, scones will be lightly browned on top and will spring back when pressed gently with a dull knife.
10. Repeat steps 8 and 9 to cook remaining scones.

Chocolate Almond Crescent Rolls

Servings: 4

Cooking Time: 8 Minutes

Ingredients:

- 1 (8-ounce) tube of crescent roll dough
- ⅔ cup semi-sweet or bittersweet chocolate chunks
- 1 egg white, lightly beaten
- ¼ cup sliced almonds
- powdered sugar, for dusting
- butter or oil

Directions:

1. Preheat the air fryer to 350°F.
2. Unwrap the crescent roll dough and separate it into triangles with the points facing away from you. Place a row of chocolate chunks along the bottom edge of the dough. (If you are using chips, make it a double row.) Roll the dough up around the chocolate and then place another row of chunks on the dough. Roll again and finish with one or two chocolate chunks. Be sure to leave the end free of chocolate so that it can adhere to the rest of the roll.
3. Brush the tops of the crescent rolls with the lightly beaten egg white and sprinkle the almonds on top, pressing them into the crescent dough so they adhere.
4. Brush the bottom of the air fryer basket with butter or oil and transfer the crescent rolls to the basket. Air-fry at 350°F for 8 minutes. Remove and let the crescent rolls cool before dusting with powdered sugar and serving.

Pepperoni Pizza Bread

Servings: 4

Cooking Time: 15 Minutes

Ingredients:

- 7-inch round bread boule
- 2 cups grated mozzarella cheese
- 1 tablespoon dried oregano
- 1 cup pizza sauce
- 1 cup mini pepperoni or pepperoni slices, cut in quarters
- Pizza sauce for dipping (optional)

Directions:

1. Make 7 to 8 deep slices across the bread boule, leaving 1 inch of bread uncut at the bottom of every slice before you reach the cutting board. The slices should go about three quarters of the way through the boule and be about 2 inches apart from each other. Turn the bread boule 90 degrees and make 7 to 8 similar slices perpendicular to the first slices to form squares in the bread. Again, make sure you don't cut all the way through the bread.
2. Combine the mozzarella cheese and oregano in a small bowl.
3. Fill the slices in the bread with pizza sauce by gently spreading the bread apart and spooning the sauce in between the squares of bread. Top the sauce with the mozzarella cheese mixture and then the pepperoni. Do your very best to get the cheese and pepperoni in between the slices, rather than on top of the bread. Keep spreading the bread apart and stuffing the ingredients in, but be careful not to tear the bottom of the bread.
4. Preheat the air fryer to 320°F.
5. Transfer the bread boule to the air fryer basket and air-fry for 15 minutes, making sure the top doesn't get too dark. (It will just be the cheese on top that gets dark, so if you've done a good job of tucking the cheese in between the slices, this shouldn't be an issue.)
6. Carefully remove the bread from the basket with a spatula. Transfer it to a serving platter with more sauce to dip into if desired. Serve with a lot of napkins so that people can just pull the bread apart with their hands and enjoy!

Brown Sugar Grapefruit

Servings: 2

Cooking Time: 4 Minutes

Ingredients:

- 1 grapefruit
- 2 to 4 teaspoons brown sugar

Directions:

1. Preheat the air fryer to 400°F.
2. While the air fryer is Preheating, cut the grapefruit in half horizontally (in other words not through the stem or blossom end of the grapefruit). Slice the bottom of the grapefruit to help it sit flat on the counter if necessary. Using a sharp paring knife (serrated is great), cut around the grapefruit between the flesh of the fruit and the peel. Then, cut each segment away from the membrane so that it is sitting freely in the fruit.
3. Sprinkle 1 to 2 teaspoons of brown sugar on each half of the prepared grapefruit. Set up a rack in the air fryer basket (use an air fryer rack or make your own rack with some crumpled up aluminum foil). You don't have to use a rack, but doing so will get the grapefruit closer to the element so that the brown sugar can caramelize a little better. Transfer the grapefruit half to the rack in the air fryer basket. Depending on how big your grapefruit are and what size air fryer you have, you may need to do each half separately to make sure they sit flat.
4. Air-fry at 400°F for 4 minutes.
5. Remove and let it cool for just a minute before enjoying.

Mini Everything Bagels

Servings: 4

Cooking Time: 6 Minutes

Ingredients:

- 1 cup all-purpose flour
- 2 teaspoons baking powder
- ½ teaspoon salt
- 1 cup plain Greek yogurt
- 1 egg, whisked
- 1 teaspoon sesame seeds
- 1 teaspoon dehydrated onions
- ½ teaspoon poppy seeds
- ½ teaspoon garlic powder
- ½ teaspoon sea salt flakes

Directions:

1. In a large bowl, mix together the flour, baking powder, and salt. Make a well in the dough and add in the Greek yogurt. Mix with a spoon until a dough forms.
2. Place the dough onto a heavily floured surface and knead for 3 minutes. You may use up to 1 cup of additional flour as you knead the dough, if necessary.
3. Cut the dough into 8 pieces and roll each piece into a 6-inch, snakelike piece. Touch the ends of each piece together so it closes the circle and forms a bagel shape. Brush the tops of the bagels with the whisked egg.
4. In a small bowl, combine the sesame seeds, dehydrated onions, poppy seeds, garlic powder, and sea salt flakes. Sprinkle the seasoning on top of the bagels.
5. Preheat the air fryer to 360°F. Using a bench scraper or flat-edged spatula, carefully place the bagels into the air fryer basket. Spray the bagel tops with cooking spray. Air-fry the bagels for 6 minutes or until golden brown. Allow the bread to cool at least 10 minutes before slicing for serving.

Roasted Vegetable Frittata

Servings: 1

Cooking Time: 19 Minutes

Ingredients:

- ½ red or green bell pepper, cut into ½-inch chunks
- 4 button mushrooms, sliced
- ½ cup diced zucchini
- ½ teaspoon chopped fresh oregano or thyme
- 1 teaspoon olive oil
- 3 eggs, beaten
- ½ cup grated Cheddar cheese
- salt and freshly ground black pepper, to taste
- 1 teaspoon butter
- 1 teaspoon chopped fresh parsley

Directions:

1. Preheat the air fryer to 400°F.
2. Toss the peppers, mushrooms, zucchini and oregano with the olive oil and air-fry for 6 minutes, shaking the basket once or twice during the cooking process to redistribute the ingredients.
3. While the vegetables are cooking, beat the eggs well in a bowl, stir in the Cheddar cheese and season with salt and freshly ground black pepper. Add the air-fried vegetables to this bowl when they have finished cooking.
4. Place a 6- or 7-inch non-stick metal cake pan into the air fryer basket with the butter using an aluminum sling to lower the pan into the basket. (Fold a piece of aluminum foil into a strip about 2-inches wide by 24-inches long.) Air-fry for 1 minute at 380°F to melt the butter. Remove the cake pan and rotate the pan to distribute the butter and grease the pan. Pour the egg mixture into the cake pan and return the pan to the air fryer, using the aluminum sling.
5. Air-fry at 380°F for 12 minutes, or until the frittata has puffed up and is lightly browned. Let the frittata sit in the air fryer for 5 minutes to cool to an edible temperature and set up. Remove the cake pan from the air fryer, sprinkle with parsley and serve immediately.

Sweet And Spicy Pumpkin Scones

Servings: 8

Cooking Time: 8 Minutes

Ingredients:

- 2 cups all-purpose flour
- 3 tablespoons packed brown sugar
- ½ teaspoon baking powder
- ¼ teaspoon baking soda
- ½ teaspoon kosher salt
- ½ teaspoon ground cinnamon
- ¼ teaspoon ground ginger
- ¼ teaspoon ground cardamom
- 4 tablespoons cold unsalted butter
- ½ cup plus 2 tablespoons pumpkin puree, divided
- 4 tablespoons milk, divided
- 1 large egg
- 1 cup powdered sugar

Directions:

1. In a large bowl, mix together the flour, brown sugar, baking powder, baking soda, salt, cinnamon, ginger, and cardamom. Using a pastry blender or two knives, cut in the butter until coarse crumbles appear.
2. In a small bowl, whisk together ½ cup of the pumpkin puree, 2 tablespoons of the milk, and the egg until combined. Pour the wet ingredients into the dry ingredients; stir to combine.
3. Form the dough into a ball and place onto a floured service. Press the dough out or use a rolling pin to roll out the dough until ½ inch thick and in a circle. Cut the dough into 8 wedges.
4. Bake at 360°F for 8 to 10 minutes or until completely cooked through. Cook in batches as needed.
5. In a medium bowl, whisk together the powdered sugar, the remaining 2 tablespoons of pumpkin puree, and the remaining 2 tablespoons of milk. When the pumpkin scones have cooled, drizzle the pumpkin glaze over the top before serving.

Mediterranean Egg Sandwich

Servings: 1

Cooking Time: 8 Minutes

Ingredients:

- 1 large egg
- 5 baby spinach leaves, chopped
- 1 tablespoon roasted bell pepper, chopped
- 1 English muffin
- 1 thin slice prosciutto or Canadian bacon

Directions:

1. Spray a ramekin with cooking spray or brush the inside with extra-virgin olive oil.
2. In a small bowl, whisk together the egg, baby spinach, and bell pepper.
3. Split the English muffin in half and spray the inside lightly with cooking spray or brush with extra-virgin olive oil.
4. Preheat the air fryer to 350°F for 2 minutes. Place the egg ramekin and open English muffin into the air fryer basket, and cook at 350°F for 5 minutes. Open the air fryer drawer and add the prosciutto or bacon; cook for an additional 1 minute.
5. To assemble the sandwich, place the egg on one half of the English muffin, top with prosciutto or bacon, and place the remaining piece of English muffin on top.

Strawberry Toast

Servings: 4

Cooking Time: 8 Minutes

Ingredients:

- 4 slices bread, ½-inch thick
- butter-flavored cooking spray
- 1 cup sliced strawberries
- 1 teaspoon sugar

Directions:

1. Spray one side of each bread slice with butter-flavored cooking spray. Lay slices sprayed side down.
2. Divide the strawberries among the bread slices.
3. Sprinkle evenly with the sugar and place in the air fryer basket in a single layer.
4. Cook at 390°F for 8minutes. The bottom should look brown and crisp and the top should look glazed.

Classic Cinnamon Rolls

Servings: 4

Cooking Time: 6 Minutes

Ingredients:

- 1½ cups all-purpose flour
- 1 tablespoon granulated sugar
- 2 teaspoons baking powder
- ½ teaspoon salt
- 4 tablespoons butter, divided
- ½ cup buttermilk
- 2 tablespoons brown sugar
- 1 teaspoon cinnamon
- 1 cup powdered sugar
- 2 tablespoons milk

Directions:

1. Preheat the air fryer to 360°F.
2. In a large bowl, stir together the flour, sugar, baking powder, and salt. Cut in 3 tablespoons of the butter with a pastry blender or two knives until coarse crumbs remain. Stir in the buttermilk until a dough forms.
3. Place the dough onto a floured surface and roll out into a square shape about ½ inch thick.
4. Melt the remaining 1 tablespoon of butter in the microwave for 20 seconds. Using a pastry brush or your fingers, spread the melted butter onto the dough.
5. In a small bowl, mix together the brown sugar and cinnamon. Sprinkle the mixture across the surface of the dough. Roll the dough up, forming a long log. Using a pastry cutter or sharp knife, cut 10 cinnamon rolls.
6. Carefully place the cinnamon rolls into the air fryer basket. Then bake at 360°F for 6 minutes or until golden brown.
7. Meanwhile, in a small bowl, whisk together the powdered sugar and milk.
8. Plate the cinnamon rolls and drizzle the glaze over the surface before serving.

Almond Cranberry Granola

Servings: 12

Cooking Time: 9 Minutes

Ingredients:

- 2 tablespoons sesame seeds
- ¼ cup chopped almonds
- ¼ cup sunflower seeds
- ½ cup unsweetened shredded coconut
- 2 tablespoons unsalted butter, melted or at least softened
- 2 tablespoons coconut oil
- ⅓ cup honey
- 2½ cups oats
- ¼ teaspoon sea salt
- ½ cup dried cranberries

Directions:

1. In a large mixing bowl, stir together the sesame seeds, almonds, sunflower seeds, coconut, butter, coconut oil, honey, oats, and salt.
2. Line the air fryer basket with parchment paper. Punch 8 to 10 holes into the parchment paper with a fork so air can circulate. Pour the granola mixture onto the parchment paper.
3. Air fry the granola at 350°F for 9 minutes, stirring every 3 minutes.
4. When cooking is complete, stir in the dried cranberries and allow the mixture to cool. Store in an airtight container up to 2 weeks or freeze for 6 months.

Nutty Whole Wheat Muffins

Servings: 8

Cooking Time: 11 Minutes

Ingredients:

- ½ cup whole-wheat flour, plus 2 tablespoons
- ¼ cup oat bran
- 2 tablespoons flaxseed meal
- ¼ cup brown sugar
- ½ teaspoon baking soda
- ½ teaspoon baking powder
- ¼ teaspoon salt
- ½ teaspoon cinnamon
- ½ cup buttermilk
- 2 tablespoons melted butter
- 1 egg
- ½ teaspoon pure vanilla extract
- ½ cup grated carrots
- ¼ cup chopped pecans
- ¼ cup chopped walnuts
- 1 tablespoon pumpkin seeds
- 1 tablespoon sunflower seeds
- 16 foil muffin cups, paper liners removed
- cooking spray

Directions:

1. Preheat air fryer to 330°F.
2. In a large bowl, stir together the flour, bran, flaxseed meal, sugar, baking soda, baking powder, salt, and cinnamon.
3. In a medium bowl, beat together the buttermilk, butter, egg, and vanilla. Pour into flour mixture and stir just until dry ingredients moisten. Do not beat.
4. Gently stir in carrots, nuts, and seeds.
5. Double up the foil cups so you have 8 total and spray with cooking spray.
6. Place 4 foil cups in air fryer basket and divide half the batter among them.
7. Cook at 330°F for 11minutes or until toothpick inserted in center comes out clean.
8. Repeat step 7 to cook remaining 4 muffins.

VEGETARIANS RECIPES

Veggie Fried Rice

Servings: 4

Cooking Time: 25 Minutes

Ingredients:

- 1 cup cooked brown rice
- ⅓ cup chopped onion
- ½ cup chopped carrots
- ½ cup chopped bell peppers
- ½ cup chopped broccoli florets
- 3 tablespoons low-sodium soy sauce
- 1 tablespoon sesame oil
- 1 teaspoon ground ginger
- 1 teaspoon ground garlic powder
- ½ teaspoon black pepper
- ⅛ teaspoon salt
- 2 large eggs

Directions:

1. Preheat the air fryer to 370°F.
2. In a large bowl, mix together the brown rice, onions, carrots, bell pepper, and broccoli.
3. In a small bowl, whisk together the soy sauce, sesame oil, ginger, garlic powder, pepper, salt, and eggs.
4. Pour the egg mixture into the rice and vegetable mixture and mix together.
5. Liberally spray a 7-inch springform pan (or compatible air fryer dish) with olive oil. Add the rice mixture to the pan and cover with aluminum foil.
6. Place a metal trivet into the air fryer basket and set the pan on top. Cook for 15 minutes. Carefully remove the pan from basket, discard the foil, and mix the rice. Return the rice to the air fryer basket, turning down the temperature to 350°F and cooking another 10 minutes.
7. Remove and let cool 5 minutes. Serve warm.

Spinach And Cheese Calzone

Servings: 2

Cooking Time: 10 Minutes

Ingredients:

- ⅔ cup frozen chopped spinach, thawed
- 1 cup grated mozzarella cheese
- 1 cup ricotta cheese
- ½ teaspoon Italian seasoning
- ½ teaspoon salt
- freshly ground black pepper
- 1 store-bought or homemade pizza dough* (about 12 to 16 ounces)
- 2 tablespoons olive oil
- pizza or marinara sauce (optional)

Directions:

1. Drain and squeeze all the water out of the thawed spinach and set it aside. Mix the mozzarella cheese, ricotta cheese, Italian seasoning, salt and freshly ground black pepper together in a bowl. Stir in the chopped spinach.
2. Divide the dough in half. With floured hands or on a floured surface, stretch or roll one half of the dough into a 10-inch circle. Spread half of the cheese and spinach mixture on half of the dough, leaving about one inch of dough empty around the edge.
3. Fold the other half of the dough over the cheese mixture, almost to the edge of the bottom dough to form a half moon. Fold the bottom edge of dough up over the top edge and crimp the dough around the edges in order to make the crust and seal the calzone. Brush the dough with olive oil. Repeat with the second half of dough to make the second calzone.
4. Preheat the air fryer to 360°F.
5. Brush or spray the air fryer basket with olive oil. Air-fry the calzones one at a time for 10 minutes, flipping the calzone over half way through. Serve with warm pizza or marinara sauce if desired.

Cauliflower Steaks Gratin

Servings: 2

Cooking Time: 13 Minutes

Ingredients:

- 1 head cauliflower
- 1 tablespoon olive oil
- salt and freshly ground black pepper
- ½ teaspoon chopped fresh thyme leaves
- 3 tablespoons grated Parmigiano-Reggiano cheese
- 2 tablespoons panko breadcrumbs

Directions:

1. Preheat the air-fryer to 370°F.
2. Cut two steaks out of the center of the cauliflower. To do this, cut the cauliflower in half and then cut one slice about 1-inch thick off each half. The rest of the cauliflower will fall apart into florets, which you can roast on their own or save for another meal.
3. Brush both sides of the cauliflower steaks with olive oil and season with salt, freshly ground black pepper and fresh thyme. Place the cauliflower steaks into the air fryer basket and air-fry for 6 minutes. Turn the steaks over and air-fry for another 4 minutes. Combine the Parmesan cheese and panko breadcrumbs and sprinkle the mixture over the tops of both steaks and air-fry for another 3 minutes until the cheese has melted and the breadcrumbs have browned. Serve this with some sautéed bitter greens and air-fried blistered tomatoes.

Roasted Vegetable Thai Green Curry

Servings: 4

Cooking Time: 16 Minutes

Ingredients:

- 1 (13-ounce) can coconut milk
- 3 tablespoons green curry paste
- 1 tablespoon soy sauce*
- 1 tablespoon rice wine vinegar
- 1 teaspoon sugar
- 1 teaspoon minced fresh ginger
- ½ onion, chopped
- 3 carrots, sliced
- 1 red bell pepper, chopped
- olive oil
- 10 stalks of asparagus, cut into 2-inch pieces
- 3 cups broccoli florets
- basmati rice for serving
- fresh cilantro
- crushed red pepper flakes (optional)

Directions:

1. Combine the coconut milk, green curry paste, soy sauce, rice wine vinegar, sugar and ginger in a medium saucepan and bring to a boil on the stovetop. Reduce the heat and simmer for 20 minutes while you cook the vegetables. Set aside.
2. Preheat the air fryer to 400°F.
3. Toss the onion, carrots, and red pepper together with a little olive oil and transfer the vegetables to the air fryer basket. Air-fry at 400°F for 10 minutes, shaking the basket a few times during the cooking process. Add the asparagus and broccoli florets and air-fry for an additional 6 minutes, again shaking the basket for even cooking.
4. When the vegetables are cooked to your liking, toss them with the green curry sauce and serve in bowls over basmati rice. Garnish with fresh chopped cilantro and crushed red pepper flakes.

Stuffed Zucchini Boats

Servings: 2

Cooking Time: 20 Minutes

Ingredients:

- olive oil
- ½ cup onion, finely chopped
- 1 clove garlic, finely minced
- ½ teaspoon dried oregano
- ¼ teaspoon dried thyme
- ¾ cup couscous
- 1½ cups chicken stock, divided
- 1 tomato, seeds removed and finely chopped
- ½ cup coarsely chopped Kalamata olives
- ½ cup grated Romano cheese
- ¼ cup pine nuts, toasted
- 1 tablespoon chopped fresh parsley
- 1 teaspoon salt
- freshly ground black pepper
- 1 egg, beaten
- 1 cup grated mozzarella cheese, divided
- 2 thick zucchini

Directions:

1. Preheat a sauté pan on the stovetop over medium-high heat. Add the olive oil and sauté the onion until it just starts to soften–about 4 minutes. Stir in the garlic, dried oregano and thyme. Add the couscous and sauté for just a minute. Add 1¼ cups of the chicken stock and simmer over low heat for 3 to 5 minutes, until liquid has been absorbed and the couscous is soft. Remove the pan from heat and set it aside to cool slightly.
2. Fluff the couscous and add the tomato, Kalamata olives, Romano cheese, pine nuts, parsley, salt and pepper. Mix well. Add the remaining chicken stock, the egg and ½ cup of the mozzarella cheese. Stir to ensure everything is combined.
3. Cut each zucchini in half lengthwise. Then, trim each half of the zucchini into four 5-inch lengths. (Save the trimmed ends of the zucchini for another use.) Use a spoon to scoop out the center of the zucchini, leaving some flesh around the sides. Brush both sides of the zucchini with olive oil and season the cut side with salt and pepper.
4. Preheat the air fryer to 380°F.
5. Divide the couscous filling between the four zucchini boats. Use your hands to press the filling together and fill the inside of the zucchini. The filling should be mounded into the boats and rounded on top.
6. Transfer the zucchini boats to the air fryer basket and drizzle the stuffed zucchini boats with olive oil. Air-fry for 19 minutes. Then, sprinkle the remaining mozzarella cheese on top of the zucchini, pressing it down onto the filling lightly to prevent it from blowing around in the air fryer. Air-fry for one more minute to melt the cheese. Transfer the finished zucchini boats to a serving platter and garnish with the chopped parsley.

Curried Potato, Cauliflower And Pea Turnovers

Servings: 4

Cooking Time: 40 Minutes

Ingredients:

- Dough:
- 2 cups all-purpose flour
- ½ teaspoon baking powder
- 1 teaspoon salt
- freshly ground black pepper
- ¼ teaspoon dried thyme
- ¼ cup canola oil
- ½ to ⅔ cup water
- Turnover Filling:
- 1 tablespoon canola or vegetable oil
- 1 onion, finely chopped
- 1 clove garlic, minced
- 1 tablespoon grated fresh ginger
- ½ teaspoon cumin seeds
- ½ teaspoon fennel seeds
- 1 teaspoon curry powder
- 2 russet potatoes, diced
- 2 cups cauliflower florets
- ½ cup frozen peas
- 2 tablespoons chopped fresh cilantro
- salt and freshly ground black pepper
- 2 tablespoons butter, melted
- mango chutney, for serving

Directions:

1. Start by making the dough. Combine the flour, baking powder, salt, pepper and dried thyme in a mixing bowl or the bowl of a stand mixer. Drizzle in the canola oil and pinch it together with your fingers to turn the flour into a crumby mixture. Stir in the water (enough to bring the dough together). Knead the dough for 5 minutes or so until it is smooth. Add a little more water or flour as needed. Let the dough rest while you make the turnover filling.
2. Preheat a large skillet on the stovetop over medium-high heat. Add the oil and sauté the onion until it starts to become tender – about 4 minutes. Add the garlic and ginger and continue to cook for another minute. Add the dried spices and toss everything to coat. Add the potatoes and cauliflower to the skillet and pour in 1½ cups of water. Simmer everything together for 20 to 25 minutes, or until the potatoes are soft and most of the water has evaporated. If the water has evaporated and the vegetables still need more time, just add a little water and continue to simmer until everything is tender. Stir well, crushing the potatoes and cauliflower a little as you do so. Stir in the peas and cilantro, season to taste with salt and freshly ground black pepper and set aside to cool.
3. Divide the dough into 4 balls. Roll the dough balls out into ¼-inch thick circles. Divide the cooled potato filling between the dough circles, placing a mound of the filling on one side of each piece of dough, leaving an empty border around the edge of the dough. Brush the edges of the dough with a

little water and fold one edge of circle over the filling to meet the other edge of the circle, creating a half moon. Pinch the edges together with your fingers and then press the edge with the tines of a fork to decorate and seal.

4. Preheat the air fryer to 380°F.
5. Spray or brush the air fryer basket with oil. Brush the turnovers with the melted butter and place 2 turnovers into the air fryer basket. Air-fry for 15 minutes. Flip the turnovers over and air-fry for another 5 minutes. Repeat with the remaining 2 turnovers.
6. These will be very hot when they come out of the air fryer. Let them cool for at least 20 minutes before serving warm with mango chutney.

Arancini With Marinara

Servings: 6

Cooking Time: 15 Minutes

Ingredients:

- 2 cups cooked rice
- 1 cup grated Parmesan cheese
- 1 egg, whisked
- ¼ teaspoon dried thyme
- ½ teaspoon dried oregano
- ½ teaspoon dried basil
- ½ teaspoon dried parsley
- 1 teaspoon salt
- ¼ teaspoon paprika
- 1 cup breadcrumbs
- 4 ounces mozzarella, cut into 24 cubes
- 2 cups marinara sauce

Directions:

1. In a large bowl, mix together the rice, Parmesan cheese, and egg.
2. In another bowl, mix together the thyme, oregano, basil, parsley, salt, paprika, and breadcrumbs.
3. Form 24 rice balls with the rice mixture. Use your thumb to make an indentation in the center and stuff 1 cube of mozzarella in the center of the rice; close the ball around the cheese.
4. Roll the rice balls in the seasoned breadcrumbs until all are coated.
5. Preheat the air fryer to 400°F.
6. Place the rice balls in the air fryer basket and coat with cooking spray. Cook for 8 minutes, shake the basket, and cook another 7 minutes.
7. Heat the marinara sauce in a saucepan until warm. Serve sauce as a dip for arancini.

Vegetable Couscous

Servings: 4

Cooking Time: 10 Minutes

Ingredients:

- 4 ounces white mushrooms, sliced
- ½ medium green bell pepper, julienned
- 1 cup cubed zucchini
- ¼ small onion, slivered
- 1 stalk celery, thinly sliced
- ¼ teaspoon ground coriander
- ¼ teaspoon ground cumin
- salt and pepper
- 1 tablespoon olive oil
- Couscous
- ¾ cup uncooked couscous
- 1 cup vegetable broth or water
- ½ teaspoon salt (omit if using salted broth)

Directions:

1. Combine all vegetables in large bowl. Sprinkle with coriander, cumin, and salt and pepper to taste. Stir well, add olive oil, and stir again to coat vegetables evenly.
2. Place vegetables in air fryer basket and cook at 390°F for 5minutes. Stir and cook for 5 more minutes, until tender.
3. While vegetables are cooking, prepare the couscous: Place broth or water and salt in large saucepan. Heat to boiling, stir in couscous, cover, and remove from heat.
4. Let couscous sit for 5minutes, stir in cooked vegetables, and serve hot.

Broccoli Cheddar Stuffed Potatoes

Servings: 2

Cooking Time: 42 Minutes

Ingredients:

- 2 large russet potatoes, scrubbed
- 1 tablespoon olive oil
- salt and freshly ground black pepper
- 2 tablespoons butter
- ¼ cup sour cream
- 3 tablespoons half-and-half (or milk)
- 1¼ cups grated Cheddar cheese, divided
- ¾ teaspoon salt
- freshly ground black pepper
- 1 cup frozen baby broccoli florets, thawed and drained

Directions:

1. Preheat the air fryer to 400°F.
2. Rub the potatoes all over with olive oil and season generously with salt and freshly ground black pepper. Transfer the potatoes into the air fryer basket and air-fry for 30 minutes, turning the potatoes over halfway through the cooking process.
3. Remove the potatoes from the air fryer and let them rest for 5 minutes. Cut a large oval out of the top of both potatoes. Leaving half an inch of potato flesh around the edge of the potato, scoop the inside of the potato out and into a large bowl to prepare the potato filling. Mash the scooped potato filling with a fork and add the butter, sour cream, half-and-half, 1 cup of the grated Cheddar cheese, salt and pepper to taste. Mix well and then fold in the broccoli florets.
4. Stuff the hollowed out potato shells with the potato and broccoli mixture. Mound the filling high in the potatoes – you will have more filling than room in the potato shells.
5. Transfer the stuffed potatoes back to the air fryer basket and air-fry at 360°F for 10 minutes. Sprinkle the remaining Cheddar cheese on top of each stuffed potato, lower the heat to 330°F and air-fry for an additional minute or two to melt cheese.

Lentil Fritters

Servings: 9

Cooking Time: 12 Minutes

Ingredients:

- 1 cup cooked red lentils
- 1 cup riced cauliflower
- ½ medium zucchini, shredded (about 1 cup)
- ¼ cup finely chopped onion
- ¼ teaspoon salt
- ¼ teaspoon black pepper
- ½ teaspoon garlic powder
- ¼ teaspoon paprika
- 1 large egg
- ⅓ cup quinoa flour

Directions:

1. Preheat the air fryer to 370°F.
2. In a large bowl, mix the lentils, cauliflower, zucchini, onion, salt, pepper, garlic powder, and paprika. Mix in the egg and flour until a thick dough forms.
3. Using a large spoon, form the dough into 9 large fritters.
4. Liberally spray the air fryer basket with olive oil. Place the fritters into the basket, leaving space around each fritter so you can flip them.
5. Cook for 6 minutes, flip, and cook another 6 minutes.
6. Remove from the air fryer and repeat with the remaining fritters. Serve warm with desired sauce and sides.

Pinto Taquitos

Servings: 4

Cooking Time: 8 Minutes

Ingredients:

- 12 corn tortillas (6- to 7-inch size)
- Filling
- ½ cup refried pinto beans
- ½ cup grated sharp Cheddar or Pepper Jack cheese
- ¼ cup corn kernels (if frozen, measure after thawing and draining)
- 2 tablespoons chopped green onion
- 2 tablespoons chopped jalapeño pepper (seeds and ribs removed before chopping)
- ½ teaspoon lime juice
- ½ teaspoon chile powder, plus extra for dusting
- ½ teaspoon cumin
- ½ teaspoon garlic powder
- oil for misting or cooking spray
- salsa, sour cream, or guacamole for dipping

Directions:

1. Mix together all filling Ingredients.
2. Warm refrigerated tortillas for easier rolling. (Wrap in damp paper towels and microwave for 30 to 60 seconds.)
3. Working with one at a time, place 1 tablespoon of filling on tortilla and roll up. Spray with oil or cooking spray and dust outside with chile powder to taste.
4. Place 6 taquitos in air fryer basket (4 on bottom layer, 2 stacked crosswise on top). Cook at 390°F for 8 minutes, until crispy and brown.
5. Repeat step 4 to cook remaining taquitos.
6. Serve plain or with salsa, sour cream, or guacamole for dipping.

Basic Fried Tofu

Servings: 4

Cooking Time: 17 Minutes

Ingredients:

- 14 ounces extra-firm tofu, drained and pressed
- 1 tablespoon sesame oil
- 2 tablespoons low-sodium soy sauce
- ¼ cup rice vinegar
- 1 tablespoon fresh grated ginger
- 1 clove garlic, minced
- 3 tablespoons cornstarch
- ¼ teaspoon black pepper
- ⅛ teaspoon salt

Directions:

1. Cut the tofu into 16 cubes. Set aside in a glass container with a lid.
2. In a medium bowl, mix the sesame oil, soy sauce, rice vinegar, ginger, and garlic. Pour over the tofu and secure the lid. Place in the refrigerator to marinate for an hour.
3. Preheat the air fryer to 350°F.
4. In a small bowl, mix the cornstarch, black pepper, and salt.
5. Transfer the tofu to a large bowl and discard the leftover marinade. Pour the cornstarch mixture over the tofu and toss until all the pieces are coated.
6. Liberally spray the air fryer basket with olive oil mist and set the tofu pieces inside. Allow space between the tofu so it can cook evenly. Cook in batches if necessary.
7. Cook 15 to 17 minutes, shaking the basket every 5 minutes to allow the tofu to cook evenly on all sides. When it's done cooking, the tofu will be crisped and browned on all sides.
8. Remove the tofu from the air fryer basket and serve warm.

FISH AND SEAFOOD RECIPES

Crabmeat-stuffed Flounder

Servings:3

Cooking Time: 12 Minutes

Ingredients:

- 4½ ounces Purchased backfin or claw crabmeat, picked over for bits of shell and cartilage
- 6 Saltine crackers, crushed into fine crumbs
- 2 tablespoons plus 1 teaspoon Regular or low-fat mayonnaise (not fat-free)
- ¾ teaspoon Yellow prepared mustard
- 1½ teaspoons Worcestershire sauce
- ⅛ teaspoon Celery salt
- 3 5- to 6-ounce skinless flounder fillets
- Vegetable oil spray
- Mild paprika

Directions:

1. Preheat the air fryer to 400°F.
2. Gently mix the crabmeat, crushed saltines, mayonnaise, mustard, Worcestershire sauce, and celery salt in a bowl until well combined.
3. Generously coat the flat side of a fillet with vegetable oil spray. Set the fillet sprayed side down on your work surface. Cut the fillet in half widthwise, then cut one of the halves in half lengthwise. Set a scant ⅓ cup of the crabmeat mixture on top of the undivided half of the fish fillet, mounding the mixture to make an oval that somewhat fits the shape of the fillet with at least a ¼-inch border of fillet beyond the filling all around.
4. Take the two thin divided quarters (that is, the halves of the half) and lay them lengthwise over the filling, overlapping at each end and leaving a little space in the middle where the filling peeks through. Coat the top of the stuffed flounder piece with vegetable oil spray, then sprinkle paprika over the stuffed flounder fillet. Set aside and use the remaining fillet(s) to make more stuffed flounder "packets," repeating steps 3 and
5. Use a nonstick-safe spatula to transfer the stuffed flounder fillets to the basket. Leave as much space between them as possible. Air-fry undisturbed for 12 minutes, or until lightly brown and firm (but not hard).
6. Use that same spatula, plus perhaps another one, to transfer the fillets to a serving platter or plates. Cool for a minute or two, then serve hot.

Honey Pecan Shrimp

Servings: 4

Cooking Time: 10 Minutes

Ingredients:

- ¼ cup cornstarch
- ¾ teaspoon sea salt, divided
- ¼ teaspoon pepper
- 2 egg whites
- ⅔ cup finely chopped pecans
- 1 pound raw, peeled, and deveined shrimp
- ¼ cup honey
- 2 tablespoons mayonnaise

Directions:

1. In a small bowl, whisk together the cornstarch, ½ teaspoon of the salt, and the pepper.
2. In a second bowl, whisk together the egg whites until soft and foamy. (They don't need to be whipped to peaks or even soft peaks, just frothy.)
3. In a third bowl, mix together the pecans and the remaining ¼ teaspoon of sea salt.
4. Pat the shrimp dry with paper towels. Working in small batches, dip the shrimp into the cornstarch, then into the egg whites, and then into the pecans until all the shrimp are coated with pecans.
5. Preheat the air fryer to 330°F.
6. Place the coated shrimp inside the air fryer basket and spray with cooking spray. Cook for 5 minutes, toss the shrimp, and cook another 5 minutes.
7. Meanwhile, place the honey in a microwave-safe bowl and microwave for 30 seconds. Whisk in the mayonnaise until smooth and creamy. Pour the honey sauce into a serving bowl. Add the cooked shrimp to the serving bowl while hot and toss to coat. Serve immediately.

Pecan-crusted Tilapia

Servings: 4

Cooking Time: 8 Minutes

Ingredients:

- 1 pound skinless, boneless tilapia filets
- ¼ cup butter, melted
- 1 teaspoon minced fresh or dried rosemary
- 1 cup finely chopped pecans
- 1 teaspoon sea salt
- ¼ teaspoon paprika
- 2 tablespoons chopped parsley
- 1 lemon, cut into wedges

Directions:

1. Pat the tilapia filets dry with paper towels.
2. Pour the melted butter over the filets and flip the filets to coat them completely.
3. In a medium bowl, mix together the rosemary, pecans, salt, and paprika.
4. Preheat the air fryer to 350°F.
5. Place the tilapia filets into the air fryer basket and top with the pecan coating. Cook for 6 to 8 minutes. The fish should be firm to the touch and flake easily when fully cooked.
6. Remove the fish from the air fryer. Top the fish with chopped parsley and serve with lemon wedges.

Shrimp & Grits

Servings: 4

Cooking Time: 5 Minutes

Ingredients:

- 1 pound raw shelled shrimp, deveined (26–30 count or smaller)
- Marinade
- 2 tablespoons lemon juice
- 2 tablespoons Worcestershire sauce
- 1 tablespoon olive oil
- 1 teaspoon Old Bay Seasoning
- ½ teaspoon hot sauce
- Grits
- ¾ cup quick cooking grits (not instant)
- 3 cups water
- ½ teaspoon salt
- 1 tablespoon butter
- ½ cup chopped green bell pepper
- ½ cup chopped celery
- ½ cup chopped onion
- ½ teaspoon oregano
- ¼ teaspoon Old Bay Seasoning
- 2 ounces sharp Cheddar cheese, grated

Directions:

1. Stir together all marinade ingredients. Pour marinade over shrimp and set aside.
2. For grits, heat water and salt to boil in saucepan on stovetop. Stir in grits, lower heat to medium-low, and cook about 5minutes or until thick and done.
3. Place butter, bell pepper, celery, and onion in air fryer baking pan. Cook at 390°F for 2minutes and stir. Cook 6 or 7minutes longer, until crisp tender.
4. Add oregano and 1 teaspoon Old Bay to cooked vegetables. Stir in grits and cheese and cook at 390°F for 1 minute. Stir and cook 1 to 2minutes longer to melt cheese.
5. Remove baking pan from air fryer. Cover with plate to keep warm while shrimp cooks.
6. Drain marinade from shrimp. Place shrimp in air fryer basket and cook at 360°F for 3minutes. Stir or shake basket. Cook 2 more minutes, until done.
7. To serve, spoon grits onto plates and top with shrimp.

Horseradish Crusted Salmon

Servings: 2

Cooking Time: 14 Minutes

Ingredients:

- 2 (5-ounce) salmon fillets
- salt and freshly ground black pepper
- 2 teaspoons Dijon mustard
- ½ cup panko breadcrumbs*
- 2 tablespoons prepared horseradish
- ½ teaspoon finely chopped lemon zest
- 1 tablespoon olive oil
- 1 tablespoon chopped fresh parsley

Directions:

1. Preheat the air fryer to 360°F.
2. Season the salmon with salt and freshly ground black pepper. Then spread the Dijon mustard on the salmon, coating the entire surface.
3. Combine the breadcrumbs, horseradish, lemon zest and olive oil in a small bowl. Spread the mixture over the top of the salmon and press down lightly with your hands, adhering it to the salmon using the mustard as "glue".
4. Transfer the salmon to the air fryer basket and air-fry at 360°F for 14 minutes (depending on how thick your fillet is) or until the fish feels firm to the touch. Sprinkle with the parsley.

Catfish Nuggets

Servings: 4

Cooking Time: 7 Minutes Per Batch

Ingredients:

- 2 medium catfish fillets, cut in chunks (approximately 1 x 2 inch)
- salt and pepper
- 2 eggs
- 2 tablespoons skim milk
- ½ cup cornstarch
- 1 cup panko breadcrumbs, crushed
- oil for misting or cooking spray

Directions:

1. Season catfish chunks with salt and pepper to your liking.
2. Beat together eggs and milk in a small bowl.
3. Place cornstarch in a second small bowl.
4. Place breadcrumbs in a third small bowl.
5. Dip catfish chunks in cornstarch, dip in egg wash, shake off excess, then roll in breadcrumbs.
6. Spray all sides of catfish chunks with oil or cooking spray.
7. Place chunks in air fryer basket in a single layer, leaving space between for air circulation.
8. Cook at 390°F for 4minutes, turn, and cook an additional 3 minutes, until fish flakes easily and outside is crispy brown.
9. Repeat steps 7 and 8 to cook remaining catfish nuggets.

Fish Tacos With Jalapeño-lime Sauce

Servings: 4

Cooking Time: 7 Minutes

Ingredients:

- Fish Tacos
- 1 pound fish fillets
- ¼ teaspoon cumin
- ¼ teaspoon coriander
- ⅛ teaspoon ground red pepper
- 1 tablespoon lime zest
- ¼ teaspoon smoked paprika
- 1 teaspoon oil
- cooking spray
- 6–8 corn or flour tortillas (6-inch size)
- Jalapeño-Lime Sauce
- ½ cup sour cream
- 1 tablespoon lime juice
- ¼ teaspoon grated lime zest
- ½ teaspoon minced jalapeño (flesh only)
- ¼ teaspoon cumin
- Napa Cabbage Garnish
- 1 cup shredded Napa cabbage
- ¼ cup slivered red or green bell pepper
- ¼ cup slivered onion

Directions:

1. Slice the fish fillets into strips approximately ½-inch thick.
2. Put the strips into a sealable plastic bag along with the cumin, coriander, red pepper, lime zest, smoked paprika, and oil. Massage seasonings into the fish until evenly distributed.
3. Spray air fryer basket with nonstick cooking spray and place seasoned fish inside.
4. Cook at 390°F for approximately 5minutes. Shake basket to distribute fish. Cook an additional 2 minutes, until fish flakes easily.
5. While the fish is cooking, prepare the Jalapeño-Lime Sauce by mixing the sour cream, lime juice, lime zest, jalapeño, and cumin together to make a smooth sauce. Set aside.
6. Mix the cabbage, bell pepper, and onion together and set aside.
7. To warm refrigerated tortillas, wrap in damp paper towels and microwave for 30 to 60 seconds.
8. To serve, spoon some of fish into a warm tortilla. Add one or two tablespoons Napa Cabbage Garnish and drizzle with Jalapeño-Lime Sauce.

Salmon Puttanesca En Papillotte With Zucchini

Servings: 2

Cooking Time: 17 Minutes

Ingredients:

- 1 small zucchini, sliced into ¼-inch thick half moons
- 1 teaspoon olive oil
- salt and freshly ground black pepper
- 2 (5-ounce) salmon fillets
- 1 beefsteak tomato, chopped (about 1 cup)
- 1 tablespoon capers, rinsed
- 10 black olives, pitted and sliced
- 2 tablespoons dry vermouth or white wine 2 tablespoons butter
- ¼ cup chopped fresh basil, chopped

Directions:

1. Preheat the air fryer to 400°F.
2. Toss the zucchini with the olive oil, salt and freshly ground black pepper. Transfer the zucchini into the air fryer basket and air-fry for 5 minutes, shaking the basket once or twice during the cooking process.
3. Cut out 2 large rectangles of parchment paper – about 13-inches by 15-inches each. Divide the air-fried zucchini between the two pieces of parchment paper, placing the vegetables in the center of each rectangle.
4. Place a fillet of salmon on each pile of zucchini. Season the fish very well with salt and pepper. Toss the tomato, capers, olives and vermouth (or white wine) together in a bowl. Divide the tomato mixture between the two fish packages, placing it on top of the fish fillets and pouring any juice out of the bowl onto the fish. Top each fillet with a tablespoon of butter.
5. Fold up each parchment square. Bring two edges together and fold them over a few times, leaving some space above the fish. Twist the open sides together and upwards so they can serve as handles for the packet, but don't let them extend beyond the top of the air fryer basket.
6. Place the two packages into the air fryer and air-fry at 400°F for 12 minutes. The packages should be puffed up and slightly browned when fully cooked. Once cooked, let the fish sit in the parchment for 2 minutes.
7. Serve the fish in the parchment paper, or if desired, remove the parchment paper before serving. Garnish with a little fresh basil.

Italian Tuna Roast

Servings: 8

Cooking Time: 21 Minutes

Ingredients:

- cooking spray
- 1 tablespoon Italian seasoning
- ⅛ teaspoon ground black pepper
- 1 tablespoon extra-light olive oil
- 1 teaspoon lemon juice
- 1 tuna loin (approximately 2 pounds, 3 to 4 inches thick, large enough to fill a 6 x 6-inch baking dish)

Directions:

1. Spray baking dish with cooking spray and place in air fryer basket. Preheat air fryer to 390°F.
2. Mix together the Italian seasoning, pepper, oil, and lemon juice.
3. Using a dull table knife or butter knife, pierce top of tuna about every half inch: Insert knife into top of tuna roast and pierce almost all the way to the bottom.
4. Spoon oil mixture into each of the holes and use the knife to push seasonings into the tuna as deeply as possible.
5. Spread any remaining oil mixture on all outer surfaces of tuna.
6. Place tuna roast in baking dish and cook at 390°F for 20 minutes. Check temperature with a meat thermometer. Cook for an additional 1 minutes or until temperature reaches 145°F.
7. Remove basket from fryer and let tuna sit in basket for 10minutes.

Potato-wrapped Salmon Fillets

Servings:3

Cooking Time: 8 Minutes

Ingredients:

- 1 Large 1-pound elongated yellow potato(es), peeled
- 3 6-ounce, 1½-inch-wide, quite thick skinless salmon fillets
- Olive oil spray
- ¼ teaspoon Table salt
- ¼ teaspoon Ground black pepper

Directions:

1. Preheat the air fryer to 400°F.
2. Use a vegetable peeler or mandoline to make long strips from the potato(es). You'll need anywhere from 8 to 12 strips per fillet, depending on the shape of the potato and of the salmon fillet.
3. Drape potato strips over a salmon fillet, overlapping the strips to create an even "crust." Tuck the potato strips under the fillet, overlapping the strips underneath to create as smooth a bottom as you can. Wrap the remaining fillet(s) in the same way.
4. Gently turn the fillets over. Generously coat the bottoms with olive oil spray. Turn them back seam side down and generously coat the tops with the oil spray. Sprinkle the salt and pepper over the wrapped fillets.
5. Use a nonstick-safe spatula to gently transfer the fillets seam side down to the basket. It helps to remove the basket from the machine and set it on your work surface (keeping in mind that the basket's hot). Leave as much air space as possible between the fillets. Air-fry undisturbed for 8 minutes, or until golden brown and crisp.
6. Use a nonstick-safe spatula to gently transfer the fillets to serving plates. Cool for a couple of minutes before serving.

Shrimp Patties

Servings: 4

Cooking Time: 10 Minutes

Ingredients:

- ½ pound shelled and deveined raw shrimp
- ¼ cup chopped red bell pepper
- ¼ cup chopped green onion
- ¼ cup chopped celery
- 2 cups cooked sushi rice
- ½ teaspoon garlic powder
- ½ teaspoon Old Bay Seasoning
- ½ teaspoon salt
- 2 teaspoons Worcestershire sauce
- ½ cup plain breadcrumbs
- oil for misting or cooking spray

Directions:

1. Finely chop the shrimp. You can do this in a food processor, but it takes only a few pulses. Be careful not to overprocess into mush.
2. Place shrimp in a large bowl and add all other ingredients except the breadcrumbs and oil. Stir until well combined.
3. Preheat air fryer to 390°F.
4. Shape shrimp mixture into 8 patties, no more than ½-inch thick. Roll patties in breadcrumbs and mist with oil or cooking spray.
5. Place 4 shrimp patties in air fryer basket and cook at 390°F for 10 minutes, until shrimp cooks through and outside is crispy.
6. Repeat step 5 to cook remaining shrimp patties.

Sea Bass With Potato Scales And Caper Aïoli

Servings: 2

Cooking Time: 10 Minutes

Ingredients:

- 2 (6- to 8-ounce) fillets of sea bass
- salt and freshly ground black pepper
- ¼ cup mayonnaise
- 2 teaspoons finely chopped lemon zest
- 1 teaspoon chopped fresh thyme
- 2 fingerling potatoes, very thinly sliced into rounds
- olive oil
- ½ clove garlic, crushed into a paste
- 1 tablespoon capers, drained and rinsed
- 1 tablespoon olive oil
- 1 teaspoon lemon juice, to taste

Directions:

1. Preheat the air fryer to 400°F.
2. Season the fish well with salt and freshly ground black pepper. Mix the mayonnaise, lemon zest and thyme together in a small bowl. Spread a thin layer of the mayonnaise mixture on both fillets. Start layering rows of potato slices onto the fish fillets to simulate the fish scales. The second row should overlap the first row slightly. Dabbing a little more mayonnaise along the upper edge of the row of potatoes where the next row overlaps will help the potato slices stick. Press the potatoes onto the fish to secure them well and season again with salt. Brush or spray the potato layer with olive oil.
3. Transfer the fish to the air fryer and air-fry for 8 to 10 minutes, depending on the thickness of your fillets. 1-inch of fish should take 10 minutes at 400°F.
4. While the fish is cooking, add the garlic, capers, olive oil and lemon juice to the remaining mayonnaise mixture to make the caper aïoli.
5. Serve the fish warm with a dollop of the aïoli on top or on the side.

SANDWICHES AND BURGERS RECIPES

Chicken Apple Brie Melt

Servings: 3

Cooking Time: 13 Minutes

Ingredients:

- 3 5- to 6-ounce boneless skinless chicken breasts
- Vegetable oil spray
- 1½ teaspoons Dried herbes de Provence
- 3 ounces Brie, rind removed, thinly sliced
- 6 Thin cored apple slices
- 3 French rolls (gluten-free, if a concern)
- 2 tablespoons Dijon mustard (gluten-free, if a concern)

Directions:

1. Preheat the air fryer to 375°F .
2. Lightly coat all sides of the chicken breasts with vegetable oil spray. Sprinkle the breasts evenly with the herbes de Provence.
3. When the machine is at temperature, set the breasts in the basket and air-fry undisturbed for 10 minutes.
4. Top the chicken breasts with the apple slices, then the cheese. Air-fry undisturbed for 2 minutes, or until the cheese is melty and bubbling.
5. Use a nonstick-safe spatula and kitchen tongs, for balance, to transfer the breasts to a cutting board. Set the rolls in the basket and air-fry for 1 minute to warm through. (Putting them in the machine without splitting them keeps the insides very soft while the outside gets a little crunchy.)
6. Transfer the rolls to the cutting board. Split them open lengthwise, then spread 1 teaspoon mustard on each cut side. Set a prepared chicken breast on the bottom of a roll and close with its top, repeating as necessary to make additional sandwiches. Serve warm.

Chicken Club Sandwiches

Servings: 3

Cooking Time: 15 Minutes

Ingredients:

- 3 5- to 6-ounce boneless skinless chicken breasts
- 6 Thick-cut bacon strips (gluten-free, if a concern)
- 3 Long soft rolls, such as hero, hoagie, or Italian sub rolls (gluten-free, if a concern)
- 3 tablespoons Regular, low-fat, or fat-free mayonnaise (gluten-free, if a concern)
- 3 Lettuce leaves, preferably romaine or iceberg
- 6 ¼-inch-thick tomato slices

Directions:

1. Preheat the air fryer to 375°F .
2. Wrap each chicken breast with 2 strips of bacon, spiraling the bacon around the meat, slightly overlapping the strips on each revolution. Start the second strip of bacon farther down the breast but on a line with the start of the first strip so they both end at a lined-up point on the chicken breast.
3. When the machine is at temperature, set the wrapped breasts bacon-seam side down in the basket with space between them. Air-fry undisturbed for 12 minutes, until the bacon is browned, crisp, and cooked through and an instant-read meat thermometer inserted into the center of a breast registers 165°F. You may need to add 2 minutes in the air fryer if the temperature is at 360°F.
4. Use kitchen tongs to transfer the breasts to a wire rack. Split the rolls open lengthwise and set them cut side down in the basket. Air-fry for 1 minute, or until warmed through.
5. Use kitchen tongs to transfer the rolls to a cutting board. Spread 1 tablespoon mayonnaise on the cut side of one half of each roll. Top with a chicken breast, lettuce leaf, and tomato slice. Serve warm.

Sausage And Pepper Heros

Servings: 3

Cooking Time: 11 Minutes

Ingredients:

- 3 links (about 9 ounces total) Sweet Italian sausages (gluten-free, if a concern)
- 1½ Medium red or green bell pepper(s), stemmed, cored, and cut into ½-inch-wide strips
- 1 medium Yellow or white onion(s), peeled, halved, and sliced into thin half-moons
- 3 Long soft rolls, such as hero, hoagie, or Italian sub rolls (gluten-free, if a concern), split open lengthwise
- For garnishing Balsamic vinegar
- For garnishing Fresh basil leaves

Directions:

1. Preheat the air fryer to 400°F.
2. When the machine is at temperature, set the sausage links in the basket in one layer and air-fry undisturbed for 5 minutes.
3. Add the pepper strips and onions. Continue air-frying, tossing and rearranging everything about once every minute, for 5 minutes, or until the sausages are browned and an instant-read meat thermometer inserted into one of the links registers 160°F.
4. Use a nonstick-safe spatula and kitchen tongs to transfer the sausages and vegetables to a cutting board. Set the rolls cut side down in the basket in one layer (working in batches as necessary) and air-fry undisturbed for 1 minute, to toast the rolls a bit and warm them up. Set 1 sausage with some pepper strips and onions in each warm roll, sprinkle balsamic vinegar over the sandwich fillings, and garnish with basil leaves.

Salmon Burgers

Servings: 3

Cooking Time: 8 Minutes

Ingredients:

- 1 pound 2 ounces Skinless salmon fillet, preferably fattier Atlantic salmon
- 1½ tablespoons Minced chives or the green part of a scallion
- ½ cup Plain panko bread crumbs (gluten-free, if a concern)
- 1½ teaspoons Dijon mustard (gluten-free, if a concern)
- 1½ teaspoons Drained and rinsed capers, minced
- 1½ teaspoons Lemon juice
- ¼ teaspoon Table salt
- ¼ teaspoon Ground black pepper
- Vegetable oil spray

Directions:

1. Preheat the air fryer to 375°F .
2. Cut the salmon into pieces that will fit in a food processor. Cover and pulse until coarsely chopped. Add the chives and pulse to combine, until the fish is ground but not a paste. Scrape down and remove the blade. Scrape the salmon mixture into a bowl. Add the bread crumbs, mustard, capers, lemon juice, salt, and pepper. Stir gently until well combined.
3. Use clean and dry hands to form the mixture into two 5-inch patties for a small batch, three 5-inch patties for a medium batch, or four 5-inch patties for a large one.
4. Coat both sides of each patty with vegetable oil spray. Set them in the basket in one layer and air-fry undisturbed for 8 minutes, or until browned and an instant-read meat thermometer inserted into the center of a burger registers 145°F.
5. Use a nonstick-safe spatula, and perhaps a flatware fork for balance, to transfer the burgers to a wire rack. Cool for 2 or 3 minutes before serving.

Lamb Burgers

Servings: 3

Cooking Time: 17 Minutes

Ingredients:

- 1 pound 2 ounces Ground lamb
- 3 tablespoons Crumbled feta
- 1 teaspoon Minced garlic
- 1 teaspoon Tomato paste
- ¾ teaspoon Ground coriander
- ¾ teaspoon Ground dried ginger
- Up to ⅛ teaspoon Cayenne
- Up to a ⅛ teaspoon Table salt (optional)
- 3 Kaiser rolls or hamburger buns (gluten-free, if a concern), split open

Directions:

1. Preheat the air fryer to 375°F .
2. Gently mix the ground lamb, feta, garlic, tomato paste, coriander, ginger, cayenne, and salt (if using) in a bowl until well combined, trying to keep the bits of cheese intact. Form this mixture into two 5-inch patties for the small batch, three 5-inch patties for the medium, or four 5-inch patties for the large.
3. Set the patties in the basket in one layer and air-fry undisturbed for 16 minutes, or until an instant-read meat thermometer inserted into one burger registers 160°F. (The cheese is not an issue with the temperature probe in this recipe as it was for the Inside-Out Cheeseburgers, because the feta is so well mixed into the ground meat.)
4. Use a nonstick-safe spatula, and perhaps a flatware fork for balance, to transfer the burgers to a cutting board. Set the buns cut side down in the basket in one layer (working in batches as necessary) and air-fry undisturbed for 1 minute, to toast a bit and warm up. Serve the burgers warm in the buns.

Eggplant Parmesan Subs

Servings: 2

Cooking Time: 13 Minutes

Ingredients:

- 4 Peeled eggplant slices (about ½ inch thick and 3 inches in diameter)
- Olive oil spray
- 2 tablespoons plus 2 teaspoons Jarred pizza sauce, any variety except creamy
- ¼ cup (about ⅔ ounce) Finely grated Parmesan cheese
- 2 Small, long soft rolls, such as hero, hoagie, or Italian sub rolls (gluten-free, if a concern), split open lengthwise

Directions:

1. Preheat the air fryer to 350°F .
2. When the machine is at temperature, coat both sides of the eggplant slices with olive oil spray. Set them in the basket in one layer and air-fry undisturbed for 10 minutes, until lightly browned and softened.
3. Increase the machine's temperature to 375°F (or 370°F, if that's the closest setting—unless the machine is already at 360°F, in which case leave it alone). Top each eggplant slice with 2 teaspoons pizza sauce, then 1 tablespoon cheese. Air-fry undisturbed for 2 minutes, or until the cheese has melted.
4. Use a nonstick-safe spatula, and perhaps a flatware fork for balance, to transfer the eggplant slices cheese side up to a cutting board. Set the roll(s) cut side down in the basket in one layer (working in batches as necessary) and air-fry undisturbed for 1 minute, to toast the rolls a bit and warm them up. Set 2 eggplant slices in each warm roll.

Mexican Cheeseburgers

Servings: 4

Cooking Time: 22 Minutes

Ingredients:

- 1¼ pounds ground beef
- ¼ cup finely chopped onion
- ½ cup crushed yellow corn tortilla chips
- 1 (1.25-ounce) packet taco seasoning
- ¼ cup canned diced green chilies
- 1 egg, lightly beaten
- 4 ounces pepper jack cheese, grated
- 4 (12-inch) flour tortillas
- shredded lettuce, sour cream, guacamole, salsa (for topping)

Directions:

1. Combine the ground beef, minced onion, crushed tortilla chips, taco seasoning, green chilies, and egg in a large bowl. Mix thoroughly until combined – your hands are good tools for this. Divide the meat into four equal portions and shape each portion into an oval-shaped burger.
2. Preheat the air fryer to 370°F.
3. Air-fry the burgers for 18 minutes, turning them over halfway through the cooking time. Divide the cheese between the burgers, lower fryer to 340°F and air-fry for an additional 4 minutes to melt the cheese. (This will give you a burger that is medium-well. If you prefer your cheeseburger medium-rare, shorten the cooking time to about 15 minutes and then add the cheese and proceed with the recipe.)
4. While the burgers are cooking, warm the tortillas wrapped in aluminum foil in a 350°F oven, or in a skillet with a little oil over medium-high heat for a couple of minutes. Keep the tortillas warm until the burgers are ready.
5. To assemble the burgers, spread sour cream over three quarters of the tortillas and top each with some shredded lettuce and salsa. Place the Mexican cheeseburgers on the lettuce and top with guacamole. Fold the tortillas around the burger, starting with the bottom and then folding the sides in over the top. (A little sour cream can help hold the seam of the tortilla together.) Serve immediately.

Chili Cheese Dogs

Servings: 3

Cooking Time: 12 Minutes

Ingredients:

- ¾ pound Lean ground beef
- 1½ tablespoons Chile powder
- 1 cup plus 2 tablespoons Jarred sofrito
- 3 Hot dogs (gluten-free, if a concern)
- 3 Hot dog buns (gluten-free, if a concern), split open lengthwise
- 3 tablespoons Finely chopped scallion
- 9 tablespoons (a little more than 2 ounces) Shredded Cheddar cheese

Directions:

1. Crumble the ground beef into a medium or large saucepan set over medium heat. Brown well, stirring often to break up the clumps. Add the chile powder and cook for 30 seconds, stirring the whole time. Stir in the sofrito and bring to a simmer. Reduce the heat to low and simmer, stirring occasionally, for 5 minutes. Keep warm.
2. Preheat the air fryer to 400°F.
3. When the machine is at temperature, put the hot dogs in the basket and air-fry undisturbed for 10 minutes, or until the hot dogs are bubbling and blistered, even a little crisp.
4. Use kitchen tongs to put the hot dogs in the buns. Top each with a ½ cup of the ground beef mixture, 1 tablespoon of the minced scallion, and 3 tablespoons of the cheese. (The scallion should go under the cheese so it superheats and wilts a bit.) Set the filled hot dog buns in the basket and air-fry undisturbed for 2 minutes, or until the cheese has melted.
5. Remove the basket from the machine. Cool the chili cheese dogs in the basket for 5 minutes before serving.

www.ingramcontent.com/pod-product-compliance
Ingram Content Group UK Ltd.
Pitfield, Milton Keynes, MK11 3LW, UK
UKHW051132260726
13967UKWH00010B/3011

9 781803 200262